MANAGING CHANGE IN VOLUNTARY ORGANIZATIONS

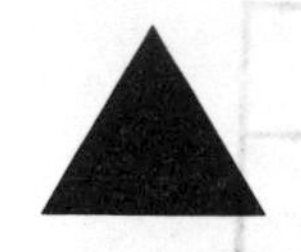

MANAGING CHANGE IN VOLUNTARY ORGANIZATIONS

A Guide to Practice

Nigel Gann

Open University Press
Buckingham • Philadelphia

Open University Press
Celtic Court
22 Ballmoor
Buckingham
MK18 1XW

email: enquiries@openup.co.uk
world wide web: http://www.openup.co.uk

and
325 Chestnut Street
Philadelphia, PA19106, USA

First Published 1996
Reprinted 1998

A catalogue record of this book is available from the British Library

ISBN 0 335 19621 7 (pb) 0 335 19622 5 (hb)

Library of Congress Cataloging-in-Publication Data
Gann, Nigel, 1948–
Managing change in voluntary organizations : a guide to practice / Nigel Gann.
p. cm.
Includes bibliographical references and index.
ISBN 0-335-19622-5 (hardback). — ISBN 0-335-19621-7 (pbk.)
1. Associations, institutions, etc.—Great Britain—Management. 2. Voluntarism—Great Britain—Management. 3. Volunteers—Great Britain—Management. 4. Organizational change—Great Britain. I. Title.
HN400.V64035 1996
361.3′7′06′041—dc20 96–8788
CIP

Typeset by Graphicraft Typesetters Ltd, Hong Kong
Printed in Great Britain by St Edmundsbury Press Ltd,
Bury St Edmunds, Suffolk

CONTENTS

PREFACE

This book has grown out of a number of support projects undertaken between 1992 and 1995, which involved the author working with voluntary organizations which provide community care, principally in the West Midlands. The book focuses upon the lessons learned from two contrasting projects. The first, involving twenty-two voluntary groups working in the field of community care, was initiated and funded by Sandwell Metropolitan Borough Council, in order to support new arrangements for funding the delivery of care services. The aim of the project was to familiarize all twenty-two organizations with the essential skills required to run a contract as opposed to receiving a grant; for example, by separating out core and service delivery costs, by achieving workable current and forward budgets, by debating and preparing development plans.

The second project was initiated by one of the organizations, the Victoria Visiting Venture based in Smethwick, over a longer period of time. It was intended to be a reconstruction project, turning the group from a traditional visiting service, predominantly dependent upon volunteers, into a professional service delivering needs-led homecare services with paid, trained workers under the direction of a 'professional' board, which would rival any private or public service for quality and value. The two projects were separate, but impinged upon each other. Both, however, were predicated upon the concept of, and the need for, substantial change in the way in which voluntary organizations operate.

The book also draws on work by the author with a number of other agencies, both local and national, which have had to evolve in response to major changes in the culture of the voluntary sector over the last 10 years or more. Most of this work has been with smaller, local organizations, or with local branches of national organizations – the sort of projects that do not have the resources to employ large staff or consultants. Many of the model procedures and other materials in the book were compiled for such agencies.

Many of the ideas in this book have been developed with the manager of the Victoria Visiting Venture, Elaine Lodder, to whom I am very grateful. Without her work and commitment, together with her chair, Roger Page, and vice chair, Sue Smithson, few of the developments drawn upon would have occurred. I am also grateful to the other voluntary organizations in Sandwell that formed part of the development project, and members and officers of the Borough Council: Councillor Fred Smith (Chair), Dave Martin (Acting Director) and Tricia Martyn of Social Services; Councillor Steve Eling, John Sutton and Helen Ball of Community Development; and many others, too numerous to mention.

Professor Colin Fletcher of the University of Wolverhampton has given invaluable help and advice throughout the work. Much of the group training work was done in partnership with my colleague Paddy O'Brien. She is largely responsible for the work on appraisal and on codes of conduct, as well as being a source of advice and support throughout. Again, without her, this book would not exist. Also, my thanks to Dr Graham Stokes, who provided a comprehensive training programme on all aspects of delivering care services to older people with dementia. I am grateful to Alan Lawrie and the Directory of Social Change for permission to reproduce the chart of quality components (Fig. 6.1).

Cathy Wood has lived with the work for five years, and borne much of the burden of the production of the book. Without her, the work would not have taken place.

INTRODUCTION: THE NATURE OF VOLUNTARY ORGANIZATIONS

- ▲ What voluntary organizations are
- ▲ The need for change – five issues
- ▲ The distinctive features of the voluntary sector
- ▲ Changes in the context
- ▲ Pressures on the voluntary sector
- ▲ The advantages of the voluntary sector

Voluntary work is one of the greatest endeavours to which people commit themselves. It harbours an enormous variety of activity, and much of it is altruistic. Can we speak of a generic voluntary organization? What do voluntary organizations have in common? And are these common features stronger in bringing them together than their differences are in keeping them apart?

Voluntary organizations are creatures of their times: they reflect the structures of their times and the preoccupations of their times. Although of varying size and with a variety of intentions, they share certain commonalities, particularly in their aims. They are philanthropic and well-intentioned. They aim to improve the quality of life, of individuals or of communities. And they are governed by people with a vision of service. They can be pressure groups, campaigning organizations or groups that have moved into delivering a service. But they have ideals and a mission. In common with their times, they have to change, and this book aims to describe what happens when voluntary organizations change, how they can control these changes, how they can retain their fundamental aims and objectives, and how they can keep up with the times in which they live.

In addressing change, voluntary organizations need to consider five key issues: (1) the management committee, (2) quality, (3) policies and procedures, (4) the post-entrepreneurial unit and (5) networking, cooperation and federation.

1 *The management committee*. Management committees, boards of trustees, boards of directors, all exist to oversee the strategic management of an organization. Yet many members of boards are unaware of their legal responsibilities, or of their duties in managing the organization, or in securing the optimum service for clients/users. To cope with changing circumstances, voluntary organizations must ensure that their management committees are adequately equipped for the new world.
2 *Quality*. Quality management offers opportunities for lay boards/committees to provide expertise, and to monitor and evaluate the work of an organization, while remaining distanced from day-to-day management and implementation of policy performed by paid staff.
3 *Policies and procedures*. The word 'organization' assumes a degree of consistency and system in the way processes are managed. Agreed policies and procedures which are regularly reviewed offer homogeneity of approach and an organizational 'character'.
4 *The post-entrepreneurial unit*. The independence, tending towards isolationism, endemic in the voluntary sector has to be broken down. Organizations have to consider their role and contribution within the entire network of provision by the public and private sectors.
5 *Federation*. The future of high-quality care is dependent upon whole-sector approaches towards advocacy, provision and evaluation. This may imply a threat to the voluntary sector's distinctive character.

What is it, then, that makes a voluntary organization distinctive?

Voluntary organizations are not essentially different in their functions to any other managed structures with a purpose. While differences have been suggested (for example, that public and voluntary sector organizations share goal ambiguity, that is, that neither profit nor mere survival can be organizational ends in themselves; and an ambiguity in the relationship between input, output and outcome, that is, that 'success' is not a simple equation of costs and benefits), the lack of clarity in the process by which tasks lead to a product is probably common to all goods and service producers. While the source of their funding may be different to that of the private sector, and while they may be held accountable to different people from the public sector, the *raison d'être* of voluntary organizations is much the same – to provide what people need at the best quality and at a manageable cost. Whether this is a change in status from the voluntary organizations of the 1970s and 1980s is arguable. It may certainly feel different to those involved. In 1988, Charles Handy wrote that 'Voluntary organizations are not businesses'. For most of us, this is demonstrably no longer the case. Voluntary organizations are businesses, but perhaps they always were. With regard to that part of the voluntary sector with which this book is most concerned, there have been significant changes in the environment within which voluntary organizations work. These include:

1 A shift in the role of local authorities away from service provision and towards the enablement of voluntary and private organizations as providers.
2 A reduction in the amount of 'untied' funds available to local authorities.
3 A shift towards project- or programme-based funding of development work

by national government through local authorities (e.g. through Economic Development Corporations, Urban Programme, City Challenge and Single Regeneration Fund schemes).
4 An increased emphasis on the use of modern management techniques in local government, leading to similar expectations of voluntary organizations funded by local authorities (e.g. in the use of monitoring and evaluation, staff appraisal, strategic and development plans, etc.).
5 A worsening of the social problems of homelessness and unemployment, and an increase in the proportion of the population over the age of 65.
6 An increasing secularization of society while much voluntary work is provided by religious groups. For example, in one local authority studied, some 20 per cent of voluntary organizations involved in community care were affiliated to religious groups, and others used a church or other religious premises.

In sum, there is far greater perceived pressure upon the voluntary sector to produce demonstrable results which can be measured against explicit targets adopted by the funding agencies. More indirect pressures upon the voluntary sector include:

1 Continued pressure upon the private sector services, evidenced by mergers of financial institutions leading to closure of local branches, 'privatization' of membership of 'friendly' organizations such as building societies, trends towards the more large-scale, such as out-of-town shopping facilities, etc.
2 The impact of technological advances such as computers, mobile telephones and fax machines, requiring instant or very quick responses, all of which increase pressure and create stress.
3 The availability of, and demand for, formal qualifications and accreditations for staff, such as National Vocational Qualifications.
4 The accreditation of organizations, such as British and European Standards, Investors in People, and local 'Approved Lists' of service suppliers.
5 The identification of funding in kind by local authorities, such as rent-free premises and the secondment of staff.
6 'Competition' with directly funded non-governmental organizations, such as City Challenge and Economic Development Corporations.

All of these pressures, direct and indirect, have the effect of formalizing the voluntary sector, requiring it to perform more like, and be measured directly against, the private and public sectors. The voluntary sector has, therefore – perhaps belatedly for some – become subject to the trends observed elsewhere. But it is important to identify how the sector might deal with these changes in its own characteristic manner, rather than be swept along by the requirements, and the assumptions, of the other sectors.

The benefits of these changes are perhaps underplayed by those who maintain that change is a negative and stressful experience that deskills the people who are subject to it, those who impose it and those who live with the consequences of it. But it would be difficult to convince the recipients of social welfare – the elderly, disabled people, the poor – that

Table 1.1 Changes in social organization

	Pre-eighteenth century	*Eighteenth, nineteenth and early twentieth centuries*	*Late twentieth and twenty-first centuries*
Production	Agrarian	Industrial	Informational
Family structures	Extended	Nuclear	Multiple
Occupation	Subsistence	Jobs and linear careers	Multi-skill work
Communications	Rural	Urban/suburban	International
Dominant information	Local	National	Global

positive changes could not have been made to the systems operating during the 1980s.

If the single distinctive feature of voluntary organizations is that they are value-driven, it may be that they are uniquely qualified to survive periods of rapid change. If Toffler's (1970, 1980) idea of the 'demassification' of society and its operations is correct, it is difficult to see how the usual instruments of service provision could have survived this process unscathed. If the evolution described by Toffler (Table 1.1 adapts this) is correct, it is possible that the voluntary sector has some in-built advantages.

The voluntary sector has a unique ability to collect and disseminate information in a way that is quite free of political or commercial considerations. The information used by local and national government, and by 'business', is characteristically partial, in that it largely concerns the interests of its end-user. The information collected by the voluntary sector, which tends to be concerned with potential user groups, is more likely to have only the interests of those user groups at heart. The information is therefore likely to be far more discriminating, relevant, purposeful and focused.

The change in the nature of family and social relationships may lead to more individual, and more individualistic, lives. This may result in a greater incidence of loneliness. However, it will tend to favour organizations better geared to individualistic – even idiosyncratic – structures and styles of working. Small, mainly single-purpose organizations, with styles of work and service delivery founded upon individualized ways of thinking, and accustomed to a needs-led approach, will absorb and exploit the talents of the individual more effectively than will corporate giants. The voluntary sector will also, of course, find that its care work, its campaigning and its advocacy, its ability to adapt to new decision-making structures, and its ability to command some access to, and some influence upon, political networks, are uniquely placed to deal with the emerging social phenomena of the twenty-first century.

Working in the voluntary sector has usually demanded a flexible approach. There has been less of a tendency to spend a whole working career within one organization, and one can now observe considerable movement of staff between the private, public and voluntary sectors. The styles of work now being promulgated in the re-engineered organizations of the 1990s have been common in voluntary organizations for some years: an ability to move between direct service delivery, administration and management; a multi-skilled approach encompassing 'people skills'; information-gathering; negotiation; monitoring and evaluation, all have been part of the effective voluntary sector worker's curriculum vitae for some time now. In particular, the distinctive expectations that the voluntary sector has because of its direct accountability to users and funders is likely to become an even more significant strength.

The internationalization of communications has already raised the public profile of the voluntary sector. Issues which can only be addressed within an international context, such as the environment and poverty, have helped to bring voluntary organizations into the forefront of public consciousness. International environmental and relief events not only grab the attention, but offer opportunities to develop expertise in cooperative working across national and local boundaries.

Global information networks offer vast opportunities to voluntary organizations in demonstrating the applicability of experience elsewhere. It is now commonplace to use practice and research from the USA when developing practice in penal reform and education in the UK. Programmes in elderly care, the treatment of disabilities, and so on, can all be informed by the greater availability of research reports. The increased ability of the voluntary sector to turn around its style of work in a short time in response to experience is likely to give it a head start in developing new models of service delivery.

This is a deliberately optimistic view of the impact of change on the voluntary sector. It is likely that the sector already has an advantage regarding the specific developments foreseen by management 'gurus':

- Permanent employment of only a small core of (mainly managerial) staff.
- Sessional/contract staff providing direct service delivery where appropriate; this will require new systems for developing the commitment to values which the voluntary sector has claimed as its own speciality. For example, commitment may be developed to the *service* rather than to the organization, and to the line manager rather than to the organizational hierarchy. This will have implications for induction, initial and in-service training, and communication of the overall mission.
- A consequent looser relationship with individuals (advisers and consultants) providing specialist expertise on a contract basis.
- In the field of community care, a concentration on dealing with generic issues; that is, providing a service (such as residential or domiciliary support) as opposed to dealing with a specific manifestation of disability (such as dementia or physical disability).
- The cultivation of multiple-purchasers, social services departments, health authorities, other voluntary organizations and private individuals [already in some areas, a pattern is emerging where voluntary organizations may manage each others' contracts, both temporarily (e.g. to cover maternity

leave) and permanently (e.g. where ownership of a workforce with a particular expertise is recognized)], leading to
- looser links with a greater range of agencies, perhaps leading to
- more structured networking or even federation, with the grouping of voluntary organizations allowing maintenance of individual identity, alongside the growth of an overarching supply agency.

Throughout this book, we will look at ways in which voluntary organizations are changing in an attempt to improve the quality of their service, in order to cope with the changes in their funding and to manage the new expectations of provision.

TOWARDS A CONTRACT CULTURE

▲ The contract culture
▲ The voluntary sector and local government
▲ From grants to contracts

The contract culture

Of all the changes that voluntary organizations are experiencing, in response to the pressures discussed in Chapter 1, the one which impinges most upon managers is the advance of 'the contract culture'. In summarizing the extensive consultation, investigation and legislation leading to the NHS and Community Care Act 1990, Wistow *et al.* (1994) write: 'It would . . . be misleading to understate the "cultural" revolution which this legislation implies for traditional ways of working'. Of course, these changes meant as much or more for the personnel in social services departments:

> . . . one of the most fundamental aspects of this revolution is the development by social services departments (SSDs) of purchasing and contracting functions within what has increasingly come to be described as a social care market . . . This, in turn, implied a knowledge and skills base almost entirely lacking in the personal social services; it was also incompatible with many of the dominant political and professional values that had shaped their organization and management.
>
> (Wistow *et al.* 1994: 2–3)

This period of very rapid transformation followed a lengthy period of time during which exhortations to social services departments to move towards a policy of care in the community were substantially forestalled by, among other things, the arrangements which allowed for the payment of benefits to those in institutionalized residential care, but not in their own homes. The Griffiths Report (1988) staked out the territory which the reforms of the 1990s were to occupy:

- the end of non-cash-limited funding for residential care through the benefits system;

- the transfer to local government of responsibility for residential, as well as for domiciliary, care;
- the introduction of a care process involving discrete stages of service delivery comprising referral, assessment, prescription, provision and review;
- the development of the mixed economy, with local authorities acting as the principal enablers and purchasers;
- the division between purchasers (SSDs) and providers (largely the private and voluntary sectors).

On a more ideological level, the recommended reforms would also allow the emphasis to shift to enable people, wherever possible, to live in their own homes, to allow people to make choices about the nature of the care they receive, and to establish forums where the consumer's voice could be heard. Between the publication of the Government White Paper *Caring for People* (HMSO 1989), which led to the enactment of the NHS and Community Care Bill in 1990, and the full implementation of the Act in 1993, SSDs were obliged to shift from effectively being the sole providers of care to partners in the provision of care. It was the new character of SSDs – as enablers and as guarantors for provision made by other agencies – that dictated the need for contracts, as opposed to grant aid, to form the basis of the relationship between them and voluntary sector providers.

As Wistow *et al.* (1994) illustrate, until 1991 the independent sector was a marginal factor in the local authority financing of provision. In that year, local authorities paid less than 7 per cent of their total expenditure on care to private and voluntary organizations in the form of grants or contracts (although there was substantial 'topping-up' in the form of seconded staff, rent-free premises and other resources). While this total disguises some variations between categories of care (e.g. work with younger physically disabled people was heavily contracted out) and some variation between types of authority (e.g. Labour and metropolitan authorities were least likely to contract out), it can be seen that relationships with other providers were largely a peripheral concern to SSDs. In contrast, the transfer of funds from central to local government to cover the cost of the new responsibilities was subject to the condition that 85 per cent of all funding was to be spent in the independent sector. This requirement had analogies in other fields. In education, for example, increasingly large proportions of local government funding had to be delegated to schools, whether they remained in the local system or 'opted out' as grant-maintained schools.

The voluntary sector and local government

Meanwhile, the voluntary sector had been experiencing considerable hardship itself. Local authority funded organizations throughout the country were subject to various forms of restraint, often starting with a freeze on growth, followed by no allowance for inflation, followed in turn by clawback of interest earnings on block grant income. The shift towards project- or programme-based funding noted in Chapter 1 meant that many grant allocations were time-limited. Whereas previously the cost of maintaining such projects was almost invariably absorbed into revenue funding at the end of their time, this could no longer be assumed. Although voluntary sector funding was only a small part of social services expenditure, it was seen as the most expendable. Voluntary organizations were more likely to provide day as opposed to residential care, and were more likely to specialize in campaigning, advocacy and in ethnic minority provision – areas which, while seen as worthy, might nevertheless be the most 'expendable'.

Contract funding introduced a new element into the equation for the voluntary sector. First, although contracts have always existed, they became 'the fastest growing component of statutory sector support for non-statutory bodies' (Wistow *et al.* 1994: 82). A principal drawback here was the lack of experience of the lead officers of SSDs, whose role was to implement the new arrangements. At a time when departments were in the midst of reorganization in order to comply with the Children Act of 1989, a host of new expectations were thrust upon them, with a very tight timetable for implementation. Not only were there practical difficulties. Many officers (and councillors) felt that the new regime was directly opposed to their own ideology of service provision.

Community care or community development?

In many local authorities, the NHS and Community Care Act 1990 brought to a head the problem of which council department was responsible for voluntary sector support, with territoriality being a major consideration for ambitious local politicians (and perhaps for officers too). The major territorial dispute was between the fast-growing discipline of 'community development' and social services. Typical terms of reference for a community development section were:

> to extend local democracy; to empower disadvantaged communities to articulate their interests; to provide structures and resources to make participation happen; to strengthen independent community networks and organizations; to tackle problems and needs at a local level more effectively; and to assist local people to have real power in their partnership with the Council and other agencies.
>
> (Sandwell MBC 1994)

Many local authorities, however, have experienced some difficulty finding a departmental home for the concept of community development and for its supporting officers. Is community development a discrete service? Or is it a style of working to be understood and adopted in (and adapted to) all service departments? If the former, what does it actually do, and how can it avoid cutting across the work of housing, leisure/recreation and, in unitary authorities, social services and education? If it is a *style* of operation, how do staff (and members) within a traditional local government model, where consistency of coverage may have been valued more highly than responsiveness, change their approach to incorporate needs-led (and therefore perhaps not uniform) provision of services, neighbourhood control and individual empowerment? Community development is more than decentralization, more than tenant participation, more than needs-led provision. The placement of 'community development' within a separate department, a common strategy in urban authorities, demonstrates at once the central importance attached to it as a working model for the council, and the failure of the authority to find a way of ensuring that each service department is imbued with the community development philosophy. And yet such a department often became the primary conduit for the project- and programme-based funding of Urban Programme and City Challenge, many of which leaned towards community care type work. The community development philosophy was therefore simultaneously seen as being of the highest priority yet marginalized.

Meanwhile, SSDs were funding voluntary organizations, some of which clearly focused on health or social care projects, while others had many of the characteristics of community development work. Alongside the reluctance of SSDs to reduce their own centralized provision, then, were other internal conflicts regarding control of resources and methods of operation.

From grants to contracts

Similarly, in the voluntary sector, there was both fear and denial of change, and ideological/political opposition. Some saw the new regime as having the potential to annihilate the distinctive features of which they were so proud:

> Contract funding deprives those working in the voluntary sector of control over their work. It replaces the distinctive ethos and voice of individual voluntary organizations with the stifling official ideology of 'efficiency' and 'effectiveness', bringing with it a creeping commercialisation and commodification of service provision and internal management, and an increasingly craven approach to campaigning.
>
> (John Gardner, *Guardian*, 8 October 1993)

Throughout the country, the voice of small voluntary organizations, the type of organization likely to provide primary care, has rarely been heard, often because of their dependence on the Local Development Agency (LDA) to articulate their needs for them. An LDA must engage the active support of the voluntary sector, which may see the council as the major purveyor of both money and wisdom. The Labour metropolitan authorities were least likely in 1991 to contract out service delivery, many adopting a traditional, paternalistic approach to the voluntary sector, whereby a community's potential for developing its own unique voice was circumscribed.

Such is the highly centralized model of local government support for the voluntary sector. When it is added to common features of voluntary organization supervision – the appointment of councillors to management committees, the determination by the funder of both overall funding and individual budget-heads, dictation of paid workers' salaries and close monitoring of expenditure – it suggests that the voluntary sector acts as an 'arm's-length' branch of the council rather than as independent providers. The strength of this approach is that it accords a fairly high degree of security to organizations, there is comparatively little duplication of effort, standards are maintained and protected, and those services deemed by council members and officers to be of the highest priority in their own strategy are those that flourish. However, it makes it difficult for new organizations to penetrate the circle, and it can act as a brake upon innovation.

There is a powerful ethos here – hidden, but colouring the relationship between the two parties. Although this approach has an overarching impact on the growth of the voluntary sector, it does not stunt the growth of all groups involved. Some organizations, while still financially dependent, have achieved a singularity of style and have shaken off some of the constraints placed upon them.

Nevertheless, contract funding allowed a number of concerns about the operation of the voluntary sector to be aired. Local authorities could hardly be expected to enter into legal relationships with any organization, let alone those that were being run amateurishly, or just plain incompetently. Whereas the earlier relationship was just about tenable – 'We give you (the ratepayer's) money to spend for yourselves, with a few safeguards, because we must not seem to be patronizing' – there was now a clear need to ensure that trustees and management committees were educated to run their own show effectively and efficiently. Far-sighted local authorities saw this as an opportunity to empower organizations and their management committees or boards of trustees. This was predicated on the belief that voluntary management committees have both a right and a duty to be actively involved in developing the policies and procedures by which a voluntary organization operates. For many, this was a new idea. Many groups understood the committee's role as being largely supportive in nature, enabling the paid manager or coordinator to run the service. This may result in an efficient and effective service, but it allows very little opportunity to develop a strategic approach to a sector where the ability to react to current trends, whether demographic or legislative, is essential. Some management committees did not even go so far as this, tending to hold a very loose rein, if any rein at all. Others veered towards the alternative end of the spectrum, employing staff with very little scope for autonomous action, while being largely ineffective themselves. Thus, where the voluntary sector is poorly organized, with little collective strength, the individual groups too may not be geared up for action or growth or development.

There was a wide variation in voluntary organizations' state of preparedness for the contract culture. The contracting system assumes that an organization has a distinct, autonomous identity, independent in terms of planning and decision-making, though interdependent in terms of funding and cooperation. Indeed, many would claim that the strength of the voluntary sector, and its ability to make appropriate provision, is founded in its individuality, its freedom from the bureaucratic structures endemic in local government. The voluntary sector is presumed to have many characteristics in common with the private sector – it is responsive to need, reactive and quick to respond to market forces. However, this is only true of some voluntary organizations. Others, for example, do not work to a budget of any sort, and their

Patronage	⇨	Negotiation
Paternalism	⇨	Partnership
	therefore:	
Improvisation	⇨	Planning & development
Day-to-day survival	⇨	Management control

Figure 2.1 Shifts in organizational culture required by contracts

only financial record-keeping is against the application for grant aid for the year. Many management committees are not aware of their legal responsibilities; do not have a clear statement of aim; have no arrangements for user participation in management; no system for training of staff or volunteers; no up-to-date job descriptions or terms and conditions of employment; no system of staff supervision or appraisal; no systematic financial controls; are deficient in meeting the legislative requirements upon employers to have written policies and procedures in such areas as health and safety; and have no system for monitoring or evaluating the service they provide.

The change from grant aid to contracts requires significant shifts in an organization's culture (see Fig. 2.1). In considering the wide variation in effectiveness of voluntary organizations, Table 2.1 suggests eight areas of operation and three levels of development. The contract culture requires participating organizations to have at least reached the adolescent stage of development.

Considerations in changing from grant aid to contract funding

The nature and composition of the contract must be understood by management committees. A 'block contract' is most akin to a grant, in that it specifies the quantity and quality of the inputs (or facilities to which the council will have access for its clients) rather than the outputs. It enables annual guaranteed purchase of access to the facility, while allowing the purchaser to specify an estimated size of client base. Facilities such as this are characterized by a loose relationship between the number of clients and the cost of the facility. A typical example is the day centre. A specified amount of money may provide places for, say, five clients more or less than anticipated, without incurring extra costs or saving money, since labour and premises costs will remain the same. However, an increase or decrease beyond a certain number, depending on the size of the premises and the care worker to client ratio, may cross 'critical break points' in costing where, for example, the acceptance of one more client has cost implications that are quite out of proportion. Clearly, block contracts provide considerable security to voluntary organizations, guaranteeing an income which is to some extent independent of take-up rates. They also allow some freedom of movement, in that spare capacity can be offered to referrals from elsewhere, and other sources

Table 2.1 Stages of development of voluntary organizations

Area of operation	*Stage of development*		
	Immature	*Adolescent*	*Mature*
Management committee	Subordinate to its national headquarters or to a dominant individual	Aware of legal responsibilities and generally participating in decisions	Individual functions shared out; a full partnership with staff
Funding	Dependent on one source; probably initiated by the source	Some fund-raising and variation of sources	A variety of sources, probably including contracts
Service	A single service with no development plans	Some development of service and some development ideas	Strategic plans in place, costed and with action plans
Quality of service	Static	Some development of ideas	Quality of service a key notion
Staffing	Staff dependent on management committee, or dominant	Some interchange of ideas, and some partnership	Management committee and staff in partnership, with each given appropriate responsibilities
Employment	Loose informal arrangements	Some terms and conditions and job description/some review	Job descriptions regularly reviewed and negotiated; appraisal systems; long-term employment conditions
Financial controls	Dependent on one member of management committee or of staff	A partnership, with some financial planning	Financial controls appropriately distributed, with regular reporting
Development	Static user profile	Some attempts at growth and/or diversification	Detailed plans for development of the user profile

of funding can be used to increase capacity. Another example of services suited to this type of contract is phone-in or drop-in advice services, where demand is unpredictable, but can be monitored to ensure value for money and to allow renegotiation of contract terms in future years. Through such a system, the department meets its legal requirements, where users have been assessed as needing a number of day care places in a week, and the organization is guaranteed its income.

A 'cost and volume contract' specifies a volume of service and a total cost. This also offers some security to groups offering more client-dependent activities. Standard care packages and visiting services are suited to this type of contract. It allows the purchaser to buy, in advance, an agreed number of care units (say, client visits by the hour). The cost of such a service can be costed accurately because, although there may be some variation according to the distances travelled by visitors, and the time of day visits take place, there is the potential to calculate an average cost per hourly visit. There is a more or less direct relationship between the cost of providing the service and the number of care units delivered. This is equally applicable to complex care packages and those providing intensive support. Again, it is assumed that payments will be made in advance, and the purchaser needs to calculate how many units are likely to be needed and are affordable. Calculation of a unit cost is critical with this type of contract.

With 'price by case contracts', a price is quoted for each type of case or unit of provision bought on an individual basis. This is clearly the least satisfactory type of contract for providers, because it is unpredictable, with payment most likely to follow the service (sometimes after a considerable interval of time). It is closest to the marketplace demand and supply model. Although it is therefore theoretically a model that is most suited to the needs of the purchaser, it does require clear lines of communication and information within the purchasing agency, as far as the available budget and the authority of the purchasing officer are concerned. More importantly, it is more expensive in the longer term because it means that, in addition to the actual service cost, organizations have to include in the price the cost of maintaining service availability when it is not actually needed (i.e. keeping workers available, maintaining a central contact, etc.). The interdependence of purchaser and supplier beyond a simplistic market model is, of course, already recognized in the private sector, where large production industries may step in to keep their smaller suppliers afloat. However, while less than satisfactory as the sole basis for a purchaser–provider relationship, price by case contracts can be a useful adjunct to a block contracted service, allowing flexibility to the purchaser to increase demand through what is often called 'spot purchasing'. There are two instances when it is an efficient method of buying care: spot purchasing of a service offered over and above a service purchased through a cost and volume contract (e.g. an organization offering standard care packages might offer an intensive service on a price by case basis, costed at an hourly rate), and spot purchasing used to supplement a block contract or a cost and volume contract, when the number of units included in the original contract is about to be surpassed within the contract period.

While the initial feeling of many potential purchasers was that price by case contracts offered them the best deal, it was soon realized that it was as much their function to ensure that a range of providers continued to survive, as it was to buy the best available deal. The consensus now is that block contracts on an annually reviewed basis offer the best prospects for a secure but competitive service.

Once an organization understands the nature of contracts, it is important to emphasize that the composition of a contract is as much the responsibility of the provider as it is of the purchaser. It is vital to the viability of the service that contracts should be couched in accessible language and not in the jargon of legal departments. One model is for organizations to produce a draft document outlining the nature and costs of the service they provide, which can be used as a basis for a legal contract drawn up by the SSD.

Development plans are seen as an essential requirement by potential purchasers. No purchaser, whether social services department, health authority or private customer, can afford to enter into what should be a stable and long-term relationship with an organization that has no vision of the future, nor any long-term financial viability. For the organization, a development plan should comprise a statement of aims (sometimes created out of a mission statement), an outline organizational audit, a set of targets or objectives, a statement of costs (with outline financial planning), an action plan and a strategy for monitoring and evaluation.

It is usually necessary to identify the separate costs of the core structure and the delivery of services. In single-service groups, this enables a distinction between the organization itself – its management, administration, support, training, central premises costs, campaigning and so on (the 'community' aspects of its work) – and its service delivery costs (contact staff, transport, specialist premises and other expenses). In multi-service groups, it enables differentiation between the core organization and the variety of projects and services offered. One reason for identifying this split is founded in the funder's commitment to supporting and maintaining the voluntary sector beyond the mere purchase of services. Whether or not an authority chooses to purchase its services for its own clients, it is argued, the voluntary organization deserves to exist – and to make some call upon public funds – in order to deliver either to its own clients or to clients paid for by other agencies. Any other arrangement assumes a synonymity of funder and referrer which does not always exist.

In theory, the combination of core grant and contract funding offers both local authority funders and voluntary organizations the best of both worlds. The grant encourages innovativeness, experimentation, campaigning and a degree of independence, while the contract demands the highest level of service delivery. From the authoritative base established by providing services, a voluntary organization can best develop new and improved services, while continuing to lobby for greater resources.

Quality standards need to be agreed. In one borough, organizations agreed to accept fourteen areas within which they would develop their own statements of quality. Seven of these standards related to the management of the organization:

- training of staff, volunteers and management committee;
- user participation in management;
- terms and conditions of employment for staff;
- job descriptions, regularly reviewed;
- equal opportunities employment;
- financial controls operating within the organization;
- systems for staff supervision, including appraisal.

The other seven standards related to service delivery:

- a procedure for client assessment (it was agreed that this should match, although not necessarily be identical to, the assessment procedure used by the SSD);
- written procedures in, for example, health and safety, user complaints, disclosure of abuse;
- equal opportunities policies and procedures in access for, and treatment of, users;
- an agreed list of services provided in addition to the core function (for a day centre, this might include visits from health services, shopping services, etc.);
- building conditions and facilities;
- reporting, monitoring, evaluation and the collection of statistics;
- networking with other organizations.

Quality assurance assumes, at the least, the following characteristics (which are not always evident in the voluntary sector):

- people are trusted to work as professionals;
- there is a strong emphasis on teamwork;
- there is a weak emphasis on hierarchy;
- goals are clear;
- communications are good;
- everyone has high expectations of themselves and others;
- the organization is 'fit for purpose'.

Organizations are encouraged to consider appropriate *performance indicators*. While some emphasis is placed by funding departments upon the significance of unit costs, these are not, at the last, critical. Nevertheless, unit costs, the cost of overheads against outputs, occupancy rates and response times, all offer useful indicators of success. Quality standards themselves, of course, offer an agreed set of targets against which performance can be measured.

Finally, a *business plan* is essential. The term 'business plan' is used, as opposed to development or strategic plan, in order to emphasize that the prime aim of the document is to identify the financial basis upon which the organization is to operate in the near future. Within such a plan, the organization's vision of potential developments is critical, but a detailed strategic plan can follow the business plan rather than precede it, which is perhaps more usual. Organizational business plans might comprise:

- an organizational audit, achieved by means of a simple SWOT (strengths, weaknesses, opportunities, threats) chart;
- a statement of organizational aims, in the form of a mission statement;
- a set of targets or objectives, including perpetuation of the current service and some development plans;
- a statement of current and likely future costs, with an element of financial planning;

- an action plan for implementation in the current year;
- plans for monitoring and evaluation of the service.

Consideration should also be given to the respective roles of the staff and the management committee in the organization, and a strategy for developing and defining these roles.

Political structures

There is always likely to be tension between council officers and members in the allocation of funds to the voluntary sector. Council officers are likely to have a monitoring role, with direct access to decision-making structures either formally, through reporting to committees, or informally, through regular contact with other officers and members. They can, and do, contribute towards the formulation of a corporate perception of voluntary organizations. In such perceptions, certain characteristics are likely to be significant:

Professionalism. Officers and members are impressed by the way in which an organization presents itself. Where possible, this means that a voluntary organization should display characteristics similar to those which officers and members see themselves displaying – a detached business-like approach to service delivery and organizational matters. For officers, this is interpreted as giving primary responsibility to senior paid staff in decision-making and, to a significant extent, policy-making. For members, however, this means conducting the *management* of the organization in a detached and business-like manner. Both of these characteristics might be seen by the voluntary sector as inappropriate to their own ways of working.

Traditionalism. Some councils still see themselves as the major direct providers of services. While key officers and members adapt their policies to the requirements of the NHS and Community Care Act 1990, many still wish to retain the council's role. There are expectations that the voluntary sector should either (or perhaps both) continue to see itself as peripheral to service provision, or look upon the council departments as the primary role-model in the style and quality of service delivery. Many voluntary organizations, taught over the years to regard themselves as amateurish and dispensable, are content to accept both these perceptions. Others, who are attempting to be innovative, find a clash of cultures with officers and members accustomed to comparatively traditional services.

The work ethic. While local authorities are under pressure to 'de-layer', to flatten out management structures, to ensure efficiencies at all levels, the voluntary sector is seen by some officers – and perhaps by some members – as a protected area. One of the traditional characteristics of the voluntary sector is that employees choose to work for it. They are freed from many of the mind-bending rules, codes and expectations of local government, and have much greater control over the way they do their jobs. They may therefore legitimately be paid less, but can expect to enjoy their work, gaining all sorts of intrinsic rewards. Local authority work, on the other hand, may be seen as boring, dominated by systems and bureaucracy, but safe. With the safety gone, some officers (who themselves may initially have come from the voluntary sector) may see the advantages accruing to the voluntary organization employees.

Factionalism. In some councils, the prevailing views – often shared by officers and members – about the ways in which organizations ought to be managed, often contrast with cultural traditions displayed by voluntary groups. At best, this is factionalism – the favouring of one group over another for legitimate as well as unacceptable reasons. At worst, it can result in an unintentional racism. For instance, all grant-aided groups might be required to subscribe to the equal opportunities policy of a council; however, the cultural pressures which lead, for example, some Black and Asian organizations to be even more male-dominated than their white counterparts, could be regarded as anti-equality by politically conscious officers or members. Alongside a proper concern that minority and disadvantaged groups should be accorded fair and equal treatment, there may be a tendency to discount the cultural reasons for apparently discriminatory behaviour, or sometimes to condemn what are just different ways of going about business, by those groups. Political party factionalism can also be rife, as is often the case in single-party councils (see, for example, Green 1981). Voluntary organizations with a key member's support might expect more generous treatment than those without. Elected members may also have an in-built conflict between their role as councillor and their duties as committee member or trustee of a voluntary organization.

Representativeness. Understandably, elected members present themselves as the voice of the people, legitimized by the ballot box. Similarly, management committee members in the voluntary sector will see themselves as having a unique insight into the expectations and aspirations of the user. This allows them to formulate policy, which it is the function and duty of the paid staff to implement. Just how closely in contact with the grass roots local politicians are is a matter for debate. Arrangements for election or appointment to management committees vary between organizations. Whatever these may be, it is likely to be true that the paid staff of both councils and of voluntary organizations will have more frequent and meaningful contact with clients and users than will the users' supposed chosen representatives, just as a shop assistant has greater contact with customers than do the members of the store's board. There will be legitimate and ongoing debate between officers and members, and between staff and trustees, about who can more accurately represent the needs of users. But inevitably, each group will tend to see itself as having the only true perspective.

One of the key questions to be asked in terms of a voluntary organization's ability to secure and retain the financial and other support of the major funder is the extent to which it will conform to the funder's expectations. The change of culture to contracting can have some side-effects on relationships between the voluntary sector and the council. Whatever else, the critical importance to a voluntary organization of a mutually robust relationship with the funder cannot be overstated.

Actions needed when changing to a contract culture: a case study

It could be said that Sandwell Borough Council, while not one of the first authorities in the country to move towards the contract culture in the provision of community care through the private and voluntary sectors, nevertheless adopted some enlightened strategies in order to ensure that the providing base remained in place and had the capacity to grow. Both key elected members and officers were committed to a vital voluntary sector. In the autumn of 1993, the two key committees involved in funding the voluntary sector – the Social Services Strategy Committee, and the Community Development and Urban Policy Strategy Committee – formed a joint sub-committee to oversee the implementation of contract arrangements with twenty-two organizations concerned in the delivery of community care. This sub-committee received a number of recommendations:

1 There should be two distinct methods of funding for voluntary organizations in community care: grant aid from the Community Development Committee for the infrastructure costs of organizations, and contracting for the purchase of specific services by Social Services Committees.
2 Block contracts should be used to purchase access to facilities; cost and volume contracts should be used to purchase standard care packages and visiting services, where individual units can be identified; and price by case contracts should be used only for the spot purchase of services over and above existing contracts.
3 A book-keeping service should be offered to voluntary organizations taking up contracts, to enable them to overcome one of the major administrative problems they are likely to face. Ideally, this service should be offered by one of the voluntary organizations (Sandwell Citizens Advice Bureau was one of the organizations well placed to offer this service at a reasonable charge).
4 The training of management committees and paid staff within the voluntary sector should be urgently addressed.
5 Transport issues should be clarified. There was currently a very mixed provision of transport, which in particular affected day centre services. The transport used included the SSD's own direct labour transport with no charges attached for some of their clients; Sandwell Community Transport – one of the twenty-two organizations – at a basic cost to some; a group's own adapted minibus; and some private arrangements for yet other clients. A separate research consultancy was recommended to iron out these anomalies.
6 The issue of how many existing clients were to be paid for by social services should be clarified before contracts were formulated. One of the stipulations regarding the change in funding arrangements was that there should be no consequent increase in costs to the council in real terms. It was therefore important to establish what proportion of existing clients would be paid for by the SSD, and what spare capacity would remain to be sold to other potential purchasers should they emerge, or to be given

away by the organization to its own clients. This would allow the SSD to meet its legal obligations by providing care in accordance with statutory assessments. Remaining places or units purchased by the SSD but not allocated to assessed clients might then be allocated by the organization on behalf of the SSD, provided assessment arrangements matched those of the SSD.

7 There should be a clear and accessible system by which purchasers could gain information about the range of care available. In the absence of such a system, organizations would stand or fall by patronage. Such a system should include, but might well go beyond, the compilation of a list of approved providers.
8 The role and intentions of the health authority should be clarified. Sandwell Health Authority had been standing back from negotiations regarding the purchase of care, supporting only one provider. How likely they were to buy from other organizations was unknown.
9 Where support to voluntary organizations was provided in kind (free SSD transport was one example, but the most common arrangement, applied to five organizations, was the secondment of SSD staff), this should be translated into cash terms at the earliest opportunity. This arose most commonly where, in the process of 'downsizing', the SSD seconded staff on permanent contracts to the voluntary sector in lieu of funding. While this system worked for some organizations and individual workers, this was only by chance. It was an important statement to make that organizations should be free to appoint and manage their own staff. In some instances, seconded staff worked alongside employed staff with less favourable terms and conditions; in others, where disputes occurred, seconded staff had appealed to their SSD managers rather than to the management of the organization. Such tensions came about only out of the administrative convenience of the council, and it was agreed that they would be phased out over a short period of time.
10 All organizations receiving funding, whether by grant or contract, whether from Community Development or social services, should have freedom of virement within and across budget heads.
11 Both funding committees should aim to develop the contract culture with all voluntary groups in the longer term.

The change to the contract culture has more far-reaching implications for the voluntary sector than at any other time in its history. It follows that the change has to be managed. Simultaneously, the White Paper *Caring for People* and the resultant legislation, as we have seen, has revolutionized the work of social services departments. In all council areas, but especially where voluntary sector organization is weak, it is the local authority that has the responsibility for managing the transition. Not only must the SSD, in order to protect all its services, support the voluntary sector, but it must also define and meet its own needs. The Policy Studies Institute identified the needs of purchasers as follows:

1 Choice of low-cost high quality providers to ensure competition at the contract stage.

2 Ongoing choice of low-cost high quality providers to (i) ensure flexibility over time to meet new needs and (ii) avoid monopoly suppliers and provide continuing competition. In addition, purchasers need to avoid 'cosy' or dependent relationships, based on perceived moral obligations and liabilities, between purchasers and suppliers.
3 The ability to ensure value-for-money, drive 'hard bargains' and contain costs within pre-determined budgets.
4 To have trust in the ability and reliability of suppliers.
5 To exercise control over who is served and how.
6 To maintain standards and accountability via easily applied, common procedures.
7 To keep transaction costs low and, more generally, to achieve managerial and administrative efficiency throughout the contracting process from initial selection to ongoing maintenance of standards.

(Leat 1993: 43)

It is self-evident that these conditions will not arise spontaneously. Their provision is being managed by a number of local authorities. In others, however, a short-sighted approach has been adopted. Many local councils have seen themselves as bystanders, allowing the voluntary and private sectors to fight it out amongst themselves, awaiting the opportunity – it has to be presumed – to pick out and work with the survivors. What the service needs is not so much competition as variety. Its absence will be to the disadvantage of the purchaser, as much as to the detriment of the providing sector and, ultimately, to the concept of client choice and quality of service.

PEOPLE AND CHANGE

- ▲ Management committees
- ▲ Staff
- ▲ Accountability
- ▲ Representation
- ▲ Conduct of management committees
- ▲ Training

Management committees

Is there anything worthwhile to say that has not yet been written or said about management committees? They have been the focus of research, training handbooks, statistical dismemberment and legal speculation. But they cover a huge range of organizations and backgrounds. There can be very few generalizations. In the early 1980s, a small study reported on the formal requirements, and the actual perceptions, of the duties of management committee members (Harris 1984). The formal duties were listed as the securing of resources, appointment and support of staff, legal duties of trustees, providing a representative 'face' for the agency and the formulation of policy. In none of these areas of responsibility, however, was the actual discharge of duties seen as anything more than notional. Staff conducted the organization – and expected to conduct it, and this perception was encouraged by the attitude and behaviour of the volunteer committee:

> However, no general staff were resentful about this since they did not expect more active involvement. Indeed, it seemed that a self-fulfilling cycle of expectations had been established between committees and staff, such that staff did not expect to share problems and decisions with their Committees, and Committees did not see any need to encourage staff to do so.
>
> (Harris 1984: 17)

This report predates the common use of contracting arrangements, so Harris is able to add that 'as it was not entirely clear who was finally accountable for the work output of local units, management committees were rarely forced to be closely involved in the agency's work'.

Since 1984, as we saw in Chapter 1, the national and local scene has changed.

This is reflected in the pressures upon management committees to adopt a more proactive role, in line with the recognition of their legal responsibilities. This pressure has come from a general tightening up within the charity world, signified by the Charities Act 1993. This affirmed the role of the Charity Commissioners as furthering the work of charities 'by giving advice and information and checking abuses'. The booklet entitled *Responsibilities of Charity Trustees* (Charity Commissioners 1993) emphasizes the contribution which trustees are expected to make to the charity, their legal duties and their liabilities. Meanwhile, a more substantial piece of work by the National Council for Voluntary Organizations (NCVO), in partnership with the Charity Commission, spells out the advice, support and training needed for trustees. These comprise 'the organisational context, legal responsibilities, financial responsibilities, personnel responsibilities, property responsibilities, strategic planning and evaluation, strategic management and accountability, and working structures and relationships' (NCVO 1992). So the climate had changed, but had the people involved adapted? First of all, who are they?

The Charity Commission estimates that there are 220,000 charities in England and Wales, with one million trustees in total, most of whom are trustees of at least two charities. The Volunteer Centre UK (1990) noted that nearly half the adult population have been involved in voluntary work, with one-fifth having served on a committee or been involved in administrative work. There is some evidence, however, that the Black and Asian communities are less likely to carry out any formally recognized voluntary activities.

People seem to get involved in voluntary organizations through personal contacts – that is, friends or relatives. There is no competition to become a member of a management committee. While about half the trustees in the NCVO survey were 'elected' rather than appointed, this seems to have been without any opposition. The NCVO's research suggests:

> . . . many people tend to drift into becoming a trustee – the Committee chooses them rather than the other way round. People see it more as a chore than an honour and often agree to take it on until someone else comes forward – then stay for much longer than they had expected.
>
> Other work . . . suggests that serving on Committees brings with it a degree of prestige and status for some people, while others find it difficult to get invited in the first place. Similar points were made to us in relation to the Black and ethnic minority voluntary sector, where we were told many people saw involvement in a Committee as a form of career development, which was often denied to them in other walks of life.
>
> Whatever the different motivations or reasons people may have for becoming a trustee, it seems clear to us, from all the evidence that we have received, that most people are not fully aware of the responsibilities they are taking on or the importance of the task they are engaging in.
>
> (NCVO 1992: 20–21)

One of the most telling findings of the research is the profile of the typical trustee as white, middle-aged and middle-class. There is a direct correlation between social class and involvement in voluntary activities, with 60 per cent of the professional classes involved, but only 22 per cent of semi-skilled and unskilled workers. Given the recruitment methods – with existing members trawling their acquaintances for people who can offer professional skills, experience or social standing – it is not surprising that the system is self-perpetuating. The *Independent on Sunday* (28 May 1995) newspaper reported a further exacerbation of these problems, claiming that smaller charities find qualified volunteer trustees harder to find 'because desirable candidates are being lured to paid positions with quangos and corporations'. Weir and Hall (1994) identified 5521 executive bodies and a further 1500 advisory bodies, tribunals and Next Steps agencies in the country in 1992–93. These bodies are run, claim the authors, by the 'new magistracy, the new lay elite of appointees': These some 50,000 appointments, which are made by government ministers, require a budget of nearly £50 billion pounds a year.

This is a far cry from voluntary organizations, where management committees identify the same problems in fulfilling their duties as anywhere else in the country: lack of time, lack of contact with the organization's activities, the difficulties of representing an uncertain constituency, and tensions caused by cross-representation on a number of bodies. The management committees of voluntary organizations may have comparatively few middle-class residents to call upon. Certainly, members with the time, interest and skills to serve on 'higher level' committees, pitting themselves against local politicians and senior officers, are likely to be in short supply. This is largely a problem of perception – perhaps of self-perception – and the key is in the recruitment pattern. If committees are looking for people to bring professional skills to their work, they are effectively seeking free labour. The appointment of accountants, bank managers, solicitors and their like to committees suggests that there is a fundamental misunderstanding of the member's role.

Management committees appoint staff to run the organization, to provide all the professional expertise in management, administration, employment and service delivery. While it is unreasonable to expect to find all the skills required in a small staff, it is equally unreasonable to expect the gaps to be filled by professionals in their spare time. Yet this is precisely what happens, and was very evident in a number of the Sandwell organizations. This strategy serves to undermine the organization. It lowers the status and the self-esteem of paid staff; it forces the committee towards short-termism by concentrating on administrative tasks rather than on strategic planning. The strategy of recruiting an accountant to act as honorary treasurer, a solicitor as legal adviser, a small business manager as personnel expert, is not only inappropriate, it is positively misguided. Few of these skills are transferable from the private sector to the specialist field of voluntary work. Indeed, there are certain elements which are antipathetic. There are four specific management responsibilities which committees have to discharge: employment, accountability (to users and to purchasers), representation and strategic planning.

In *employment* matters, it is likely that the procedures within the public and voluntary sectors will be significantly different from those used by private businesses. One voluntary organization received funding for two new posts and adopted the following most rigorous procedures for appointment.

Selection and appointment of staff

(A sample appointments procedure is given in Appendix A)

1 *Identification of a vacancy.* In the event of the departure of an existing member of staff, or the identification of the need for a new post, the first stage is that the management committee must agree that a vacant post has to be filled. It is not unknown for organizations to spot someone they would like to employ before locating the funds to do so, to find that funding is available for a post or project they are not especially committed to, or to assume that, as one member of staff leaves, their post needs to be replicated exactly. This process requires an audit of the organization's needs arising out of its agreed mission statement. For this reason, a vacancy arising often creates an ideal moment for a management committee to look again at some fundamentals: What are we here to do? Where do we want the organization to go now? Clearly, the more senior the vacancy, the more necessary this process is. The identification of need leads to the formulation of an appointment timetable, a budget for the procedure, and . . .
2 *Drawing up a job description.* This will include a job title; a statement of the post or committee to which the job will be responsible; posts the job will be responsible for; other key contacts of the job; and terms of employment, working hours and special conditions. There will also be a brief summary of the job, and a list of responsibilities or duties. Attached to this will be a . . .
3 *Person (or personnel) specification.* This will comprise a list of the skills, knowledge, experience, characteristics and qualifications which the committee will expect candidates to have. The list will probably be divided into essentials and desirables.
4 The *advertisement* can now be drawn up, and decisions made as to where the post is to be advertised – local and national newspapers, professional journals, newspapers, or other ways of communicating which will reach particular groups or communities, such as ethnic minorities or disabled people.
5 An *equal opportunities monitoring form* will ensure that the advertisement has reached all the communities necessary to enable the best candidates to apply, and in such a way that the application process is accessible.
6 *Information for the applicants* will include the job description, person specification, advertisement, monitoring form, a request for a letter of application to go with the completed form, with directions on what to include, and particulars about the interview arrangements. Details of referees should be requested here. The application form will, of course, avoid mention of irrelevancies such as age, gender, ethnic origin and marital status. It can be arranged here for a neutral adviser to remove names from the forms and letters, replacing them with a code. This enables the shortlisting panel to concentrate on the essentials.
7 The *shortlisting procedure,* conducted by a panel appointed by the management committee, begins with agreement on the shortlisting criteria. Figure 3.1 shows the sheet used by the panel to create a shortlist for a position in a housing organization.

Character Ref ______					
	high				low
Essential	5	4	3	2	1
Experience of the voluntary sector					
Experience of financial control					
Formal qualifications					
Experience of the housing sector					
Experience of servicing committees					
Experience of writing reports					
Ability to communicate ideas in writing					
Ability to represent the public face of the organization					
Awareness of empowerment issues					
Awareness of equal opportunities issues					
Reflection on the job description					
Desirable					
Starting up a new project					
Working with community groups					
Working with housing authorities					
Working with housing associations					
Working with local government					
Publicity					
Awareness of the importance of training					

Panel Member ______________________

Interview *No* *Maybe* *Yes*

Figure 3.1 Shortlisting checklist

8 The *interview process* should be designed to be sufficiently formal to be purposeful and business-like, yet sufficiently informal to put everyone (including the panel) at their ease and likely to be at their best. Equal opportunity interviews do not, as some seem to think, need to be depersonalized and humourless. It is essential that all candidates get the same lead questions, but this does not exclude the possibility of exploring candidates' answers, nor of asking for points raised in the letter or form of application to be developed. There should be a common and agreed method of recording the candidate's performance. Figure 3.2 shows a sheet used by the interview panel.

Each criterion was covered by one or more questions agreed and allocated to members of the panel, with notes to guide the panel as to where to look for the responses. Members of the panel who were less experienced in the selection process were given a half-day training session beforehand to give them the confidence to perform. Following the interviews, a structured decision-making session allowed the panel to select the preferred candidate.

Development & Information Officer						
Interview schedule						
Candidate 1: Candidate 2: Candidate 3: Candidate 4: Candidate 5: Candidate 6:	Scoring A (Very good) – E (Very poor)					
Essential	1	2	3	4	5	6
Communicating ideas in speech						
Managing new project, planning						
Networking, promoting, organizing						
Presenting professional aspect						
Line-management issues						
Empathy and empowerment						
Equal opportunities						
Teamwork/management committee						
Ability to work flexibly						
Listening/understanding						

Figure 3.2 Interview checklist

Only at this point were references read, to check out and confirm the information received in the application and interview. All records and notes taken in the interview room were collected and retained by the chair for six months, in case of a challenge to the procedure. All candidates were contacted by telephone as soon as the panel had reached a decision, and the unsuccessful interviewees were offered a debrief on the reasons for their rejection.

Employment

'Many trustees do not have the expertise or knowledge effectively to recruit, appoint, monitor and appraise staff' (NCVO 1992). Staff in many voluntary organizations will heartily endorse this statement. It surely is the case that the most serious and the most regular problems faced in the voluntary sector are those concerning employment. First, many workers, particularly in small locally based organizations, do not even have the basic requirements of terms and conditions, job descriptions and line management responsibilities. Much more rare are personnel support systems such as appraisal (one chair of a small day centre said, 'Appraisal? We don't want anything like that here. I was appraised once at work and I didn't like it at all'). It is the committee's duty – in many cases its legal duty – to ensure that its employment practices are adequate, and it may be necessary to buy in this expertise where it is not available. Beware particularly of the committee member who says, 'I run a business myself, I know all about these things'. A number of voluntary organizations will happily buy in routine payroll services, but draw the line at any expenditure on employment practice. More than most jobs, staff within the voluntary sector, whether paid or voluntary, need good career support, in-service training and development. The UK Standard, Investors in People, which will be considered later in this book, offers a framework for the support and development of staff at all levels. The very informality and resistance to bureaucracy that we often see as among the most attractive characteristics of the voluntary sector, particularly of the smaller organizations, can bring about an absence of formal support mechanisms for paid and, even more so, volunteer staff. All staff are entitled to agreed codes of practice in their relationships with their employers, to formal negotiation arrangements on salaries and terms and conditions, and to arrangements for pensions.

Accountability

It is not the role of lay management committees to replicate half-heartedly the tasks that are being done, or that should be done, by paid staff. Management committees bring quite discrete skills, characteristics and points of view to voluntary organizations. We shall see in Chapter 6 and elsewhere how these can be deployed to further the effectiveness of the service. Here, we consider the three bodies which management committees represent and are accountable to in their role. Often, this accountability is demonstrated by election or nomination from a specific constituency, but this is neither a complete definition of such representatives' role, nor does the provenance of some members rule out the duty that other members have of considering the needs of all three bodies.

Accountability to the organization

The first duty that a management committee has is to ensure the effectiveness of the organization. The specific role they might play here, and the ways in which this duty is best discharged, will be looked at later. But the constitutions of many voluntary organizations, supplemented by local authority regulations demanding representation on funded bodies, may tend to emphasize the duty of the representative to the source of his or her nomination rather than to the organization itself. The organization must remind elected and nominated members that, regardless of where they come from and why they are there, their first duty is to the organization itself. Multi-purpose organizations such as community centres are particularly prone to the type of factionalism which is fostered by the 'two of these, two of those' mentality. While the interests of these and those have to be forwarded by their representatives, this is for the moment secondary to the organization's own interests.

Accountability to users

Some voluntary organizations have user representation on their committees. But quite apart from the user representatives, members bring a unique perspective to the service, which is quite distinct from the professional view. They are likely to be:

- less shackled to professional jargon and current trends, and more questioning of received professional wisdom;
- more able to identify the significant issues and concerns for users;
- more able to take issues and concerns back to users, and develop a sense of ownership;
- more able to represent the organization to funders and other agencies in a plainly disinterested manner.

But they are also likely to be:

- devalued by professional staff both inside and outside the organization itself;
- less comfortable with committee behaviour (such as presenting arguments and accepting collective responsibility for decisions).

Committee behaviour is, of course, a strange language to learn. Handbooks frequently advise new members to learn by listening, to become familiar with rules, and to generally take on all the characteristics of the committee. Rarely are committees advised to learn from their new members. Yet committees are predicated upon certain values that may be foreign to the experience and cultures of many of the potentially most valuable participants. They are conceived upon reasonableness, upon measured decisions and actions, on negotiation and consensus. Yet these are sometimes the predominant values against which organizations have sprung up in the first place. Some of the best of the voluntary sector is founded upon frustration with the inability or unwillingness of authority to act. The sector has to be careful that it does not learn to play the game so convincingly to the others' rules that it loses its own *raison d'être*. A place has to be found for anger, polemicism and quick action, all the things which do not sit well in committees.

Accountability to purchasers

Management committees offer a unique advantage to purchasers over the private and public sectors. The overall responsibility of lay people free of both profit motive and political interest, and charged with both short- and long-term supervision and governance, makes it easier for purchasers (usually social services or health authorities) to negotiate on quality. However, until contracting is common currency in the purchase of services, it is likely that many voluntary organizations will be wary of the legal responsibilities that they are taking on.

It is useful to present the broad picture of organizational accountability in diagrammatic form for the benefit of staff, users and the management committee. One organization participating in the Department of Health's nationwide 'Caring for People Who Live at Home' project had a complex network of responsibilities and accountabilities, as shown in Fig. 3.3.

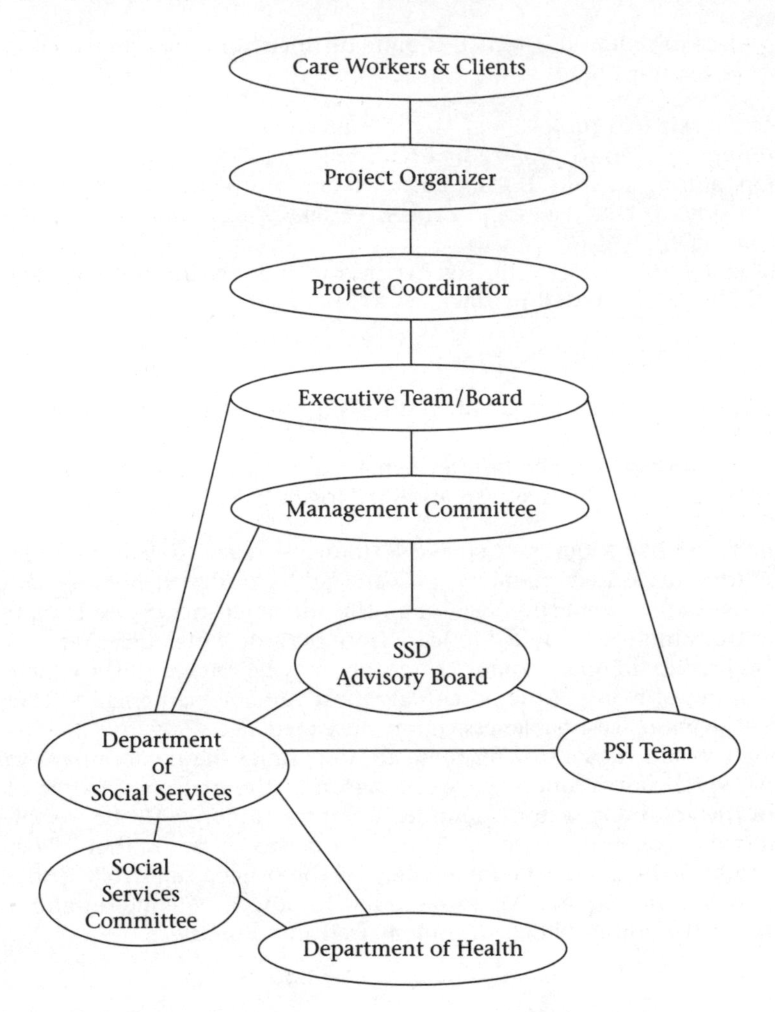

Figure 3.3 Sample accountability trail

A code of conduct

New – and indeed long-serving – committee members may find simple guidance on the major responsibilities of their role helpful. This can be enshrined in a code of conduct, as follows:

1 No member has individual authority or power by being a member of the committee, unless it has been specifically delegated; only the committee as a whole can take actions or decisions unless agreed otherwise and recorded in the minutes.
2 No member must use his or her position to gain advantage in other relationships with the organization or other agencies.
3 The committee recognizes that it administers a body funded by public

money. It therefore recognizes the need to ensure that its proceedings are properly conducted and open to public scrutiny (while recognizing the need to be confidential where individual users and staff are under discussion).

4. All members, however elected or appointed, recognize that they are individually accountable to certain bodies or constituencies. All members have a duty to consider the significance of decisions for the source of their appointment during discussion on any item, to report back to any elective or appointing body, and to initiate systems of gathering views on matters likely to be brought before the committee.
5. No member can be mandated to vote in a particular way by his or her appointing body under any circumstances, although he or she should report any views expressed by members of that body.
6. All committee members are of equal standing.
7. All members are appointed, and should act, for the good of the organization, whatever the basis of their appointment.
8. Members must be careful to ensure that their relationship with the organization is conducted in a proper and ethical manner, and that their standing as a committee member is not compromised or open to misinterpretation.
9. Members will attend meetings punctually and be well prepared, having read the agenda and supporting papers, and having considered the contribution they may make on agenda items.
10. Members will not use any information learned at meetings for other purposes, and no item designated as confidential will be discussed outside the committee.
11. Members accept collective responsibility for the decisions of the committee.
12. Members will consider what individual skills, personal qualities and knowledge they have, and put them to use for the good of the organization.

The overall practice of the committee can be evaluated using a simple format, such as that shown in Appendix B.

Representation

Ownership of an organization is an important perception by members, staff, users and funders. One of the surprising characteristics of the voluntary sector is the extent to which there is cross-representation on management committees. Indeed, in one example I have experienced, two lead staff acted as each other's chair and vice-chair respectively. The heavy predominance of voluntary sector staff can undermine the lay role of committees, especially where lay members carry with them the weaknesses listed above (see p. 29).

The role of representatives of the funder is unclear. Many organizations have both an officer and a council member appointed to serve on their committee although a number of local authorities now forbid this. The potential role confusion of officers has already been observed. Are they there to support the organization, monitor its progress, represent the 'official' funder's view, or advocate for the organization? The quality, status and commitment of the political members can also be a significant factor in the 'patronage' of an organization, while they face basically the same issues as officers. The move to contracting demands the resolution of some of these issues, and it would seem unreasonable for council officers to continue to serve on committees *ex officio*. It is also important that decisions about contracts with providers should remain with council members, ensuring that funding of the organizations within the voluntary sector remains a political decision open to public scrutiny.

Conduct of management committees

One of the intriguing features of voluntary sector governance is the wide variety of perceptions of the role by lay members. The absence of any clear definition of functions lays committee processes open to abuse or neglect, the most common form of abuse being dominance by one or a small group of members, and that of neglect inviting control by paid staff.

The management committees of mature voluntary organizations seem to have at least the following characteristics:

1 *An understanding of the role.* Members will show by their conduct and by the organization of their tasks that they have a clear understanding of their roles, functions and responsibilities.
2 *Individual functions.* Members will have taken on specific responsibilities. Some will be officers – chair, vice-chair, secretary, etc. Each job will have a job description. Other functions may be taking a lead role in (but not sole responsibility for) fund-raising, liaison with funders, health and safety, equal opportunities, personnel and finance.
3 *A team approach.* Committees will be composed of people with a variety of skills, characteristics and knowledge. One way of ensuring this might be to adopt Belbin's (1981) classifications. The eight roles identified by Belbin are those of organizer, chairman, shaper, innovator, resource investigator, monitor evaluator, team worker, completer-finisher. It is the combination of these functions or team roles that allows a team to operate effectively. While Belbin constructed teams based on a mix of preferred team roles identified by simple personality tests, it is worth noting that most people have secondary roles which they can play if no-one else is fitted for it, or if someone else on the team plays their own preferred role better. Committees might well use Belbin's roles to identify the skills which are needed in their team. Ideally, the team is constructed around these skills, but it is perfectly possible for individual members to be directed towards concentrating on aspects of their personality which the team needs. While we all have recognizable dominant characteristics, we also behave differently in different situations, and can practise, and call on, modes of behaviour which tend elsewhere to be suppressed. We can also use this approach with organizational functions. Members with specific functions like those

listed above are being asked to take on the responsibility of ensuring that that particular function of the organization is considered during discussion on any matter of policy or implementation. We accept that the treasurer or chair of finance will probably remind us when the spending implications of decisions run beyond the budget; and that the personnel officer or chair of the staffing committee will do likewise with staffing matters. Similarly, members with responsibility for equal opportunities, or health and safety, should be relied upon to have those issues always at the forefront of their minds. This does not, of course, absolve the rest of the committee from raising these concerns. But it does ensure that the issue is addressed. Ideally, such functions are swapped around, so that no one person is always charged with the duty of saying, for example, 'We can't afford that'. Similarly, perhaps, with Belbin's preferred team roles. We can practise and develop such skills, to the benefit of ourselves and of the organization. Such clearly defined benefits will also help to raise the self-esteem of committee members, enabling them to gain the confidence to play a significant role in organizational development, when incorporated into the type of strategic approach to management described in the following chapters.

Strategic planning

An effective management committee will have an understanding of the need for long-term organizational development. This will be looked at in depth in Chapter 4.

Balanced representation

An effective committee will have regard not only to its duties of representativeness, but also to the balance of its composition in terms of age, gender, ethnic and cultural background, and length of service. In early 1994, the Single Homeless Project based in South-East London, advertised for management committee members in the national press. The advertisement specified a need for people

> with an interest in issues around homelessness; a firm commitment to Equal Opportunities; general experience of working with people; expertise in finance management, personnel management, property development or housing management; a desire to expand their understanding of one of these; and a willingness to commit at least four hours a month.

The project offered payment of travel costs in London, payment of child-minding fees, and the opportunity to develop and use managerial skills and to manage strategic change. From the responses, some twenty candidates were interviewed and eight selected. This type of explicit statement of need and professional approach to recruitment of volunteers would be a conceptual leap forward for much of the small voluntary sector.

Training staff: A case study

This section centres upon three years of work with the care staff of Victoria Visiting Venture (VVV), a small voluntary organization based in Smethwick, the West Midlands. The VVV project engaged a consultant at the time when funding for the Department of Health's 'Caring for People Who Live at Home' initiative was confirmed, in 1993. The consultancy brief was in two parts. First, the project needed to have a framework in place for the appointment and employment of staff, followed by a set of documents, policies and procedures which would guide its management and development. Second, the project needed a training programme for management staff, the project board (which comprised representatives of staff, the management committee and the SSD) and, eventually, care assistants.

Few organizations get a chance to start again. Until recently, voluntary organizations and the public sector were perhaps more firmly wedded to their histories than the private sector. But contracting offers the opportunity to the voluntary sector to reconsider its mission, its objectives, its organization, its relationships and its future. And the project culture which is inherent to the contracting relationship may well offer recurrent opportunities to organizations to undertake this kind of regular self-assessment. Such an opportunity was offered to VVV.

It was agreed that the aim of the consultancy was to 'ensure the optimum effectiveness of the project's work, by raising awareness of the project's aims and objectives, and providing the management board, staff and care workers with opportunities to share and explore issues arising out of day-to-day management'. Alongside this, plans were laid to ensure that the first tranche of care assistants would have training opportunities in practical care, mental and physical health. One of the early decisions to be made by the board was that care workers would be employed on a part-time, sessional basis. This would give the project maximum flexibility. It was, of course, recognized that there might be costs in a lower commitment of staff. However, the nature of employment in Sandwell and elsewhere in the early 1990s suggested that there would be a good response, as there was. In the event, of the fifteen people initially appointed to the care-workers' register, a number already held part-time posts in the care services, mainly in nursing homes. The attractions of the different style of employment, the comparative independence offered by the posts, the level of involvement in decision-making, and the comparatively high hourly rate, led to a very low turnover of staff in the first year. By the spring of 1994, VVV employed twenty-one care workers (sixteen women and five men) aged 21–65 years. Thirteen of the staff were of Afro-Caribbean origin, four were Asian and four white European. Seventeen of the twenty-one had other employment elsewhere. Twelve had at least some basic qualification in care work.

The first set of workshops and their objectives were agreed, up to the summer of 1994. The final training programme for organizational change was as shown in Table 3.1. Practical training comprised in-house sessions on working with dementia; the management of challenging behaviour; caring with competence; needs-led assessment; working with families; coping with

Table 3.1 Organization training programme

Date	*Objectives*	*Group*	*Days*
April 1993	Establish an agreed mission statement and aims for the project	Management board and staff	2
May 1993	Familiarize care staff with project aims; provide opportunities for management and care workers to agree outputs and outcomes, and to share other issues arising out of the project; provide introductory training in equal opportunities issues; identify care workers' skills	Management staff and care workers	2
June 1993	Provide feedback on first evaluation; develop and revise strategic plans	Management board and staff	1
Sept 1993	Conduct a service audit; agree performance indicators and draft quality standards	Management board and staff	1
Nov 1993	Agree quality standards and code of conduct	Management staff and care workers	1
Dec 1993	Agree appraisal procedures	Management staff and care workers	1
Feb 1994	Agree criteria of eligibility for users (access criteria)	Management board and staff	1
June 1994	Communicate and discuss aims, skills and equal opportunities issues with newly appointed care workers	Care workers	1
June 1994	Review and evaluate work to date	Care workers	1
July 1994	Review work to date: consider the implications for the service of change in the organization; identify action plans for 1994–95	Management board and staff	1
Dec 1994	Review and revise business plan	Management board and staff	2
March 1995	Evaluate training needs	Care workers	1
July 1995	Review work to date: consider the implications for the service of change in the organization; identify action plans for 1995–96	Management board and staff	1

stress in care settings; depression in elderly people; counselling confused elderly people; rights, risks and responsibilities; and the abuse of older adults. Meanwhile, a programme of monitoring and evaluation of the service was agreed, to begin in May 1993. The organization mission statement was put together by the board and staff (the project organizer, having been appointed in the spring of 1993, joined the VVV coordinator in all these sessions). In defining aims, or writing a mission statement, one approach is to ask the group to provide a series of key concepts which they want to see represented in some form in the final version. These can then be grouped together and the final version produced. In this case the chair, coordinator and organizer listed the following words and phrases:

> Careful planning; change; growth; effectiveness; how to say what we want?; learning and growing with its clients; dynamic; was this baby really needed?; genuine thinking environment; mutual support; confidence; self-esteem; referral; information; a mixed and representative workforce; going out into the community; monitoring; training; how to identify and address needs; access of black elders to the service; imaginative challenge to the community; an area of multiple deprivation and few resources; political ideology; existing expertise; unknown needs; household word; voluntary resources; innovation.

(This list was the first occasion on which the project was anthropomorphized, in this case as a baby. This metaphor arose frequently throughout subsequent sessions, and the significance of this was explored some 2 years on.) These were, then, used to form the basis of a mission statement and, later, as a starting-point for the formulation of project objectives. The agreed statement ran:

> The Care at Home Project will provide an innovative needs-led home care service to older people, sufficiently to improve their quality of life, enabling them to remain in their own homes. The project will take positive action to promote accessibility to its services by black elders and older people with a mental illness. However, the service will be accessible to older people regardless of ethnicity, sexuality, gender, religious or political beliefs, with the aim of enabling maximization of individual potential.

In putting this mission statement together, it was agreed by the board that the key words and phrases were 'innovative', 'needs-led', 'quality of life', 'promote accessibility' and 'maximization of individual potential'. The primary objective of the first training session was to develop ownership of this statement by the care workers and, to do this, the full implications of each word and phrase had to be explored and understood. The first part of the session dealt with the hopes and fears of the care workers. The degree to which they would be required to develop ownership of the project was neatly illustrated when, in response to the session-leader's question, 'What do you think we are here to do today?', the answer came back, 'You're going to tell us the rules'. This enabled an early demonstration of the difference in culture that those who worked in nursing homes were likely to be about to experience, with the response, 'No, we're going to make up the rules together'. After some introductory exercises, the group began to explore the meaning, and the implications for them, of the key words. The results were as follows:

1 *Innovative*. It was a requirement of the Department of Health that the project should develop new ways of delivering an increased range of services, and not merely replicate, within the voluntary sector, the services provided by SSDs. It was helpful, then, that VVV had not been founded within a 'home-help culture'; through its genesis within a support service which attempted to respond to a wide *variety* of need, even though these tended to be at a low *level* of need, the organization was better equipped to approach the project in an innovative frame of mind. As we have seen, the management committee had recently embarked on an exercise through which it could maximize its own performance, so the main participants were well-placed to start from outside the mainstream of thinking about caring services. For the workers, the word signalled 'new' and 'different' approaches, but the implications of this were probably not evident until after a few weeks or months.
2 *Needs-led*. Professor Colin Fletcher of Wolverhampton University, who has supported the project, and contributed in a number of ways to its development, has written, in another context:

   > Needs do not fall into one's lap – they have to be found. Needs are weak, intermittent and separate signals which adults make when they are not sure, not determined and not in contact with other adults with similar feelings to themselves. Needs contrast with demands, which are the strong, regular and collective communications that people make about and for themselves.
   >
   > (Fletcher 1984: 38)

   The key to providing a needs-led service is in the quality of the assessment. VVV came to regard the initial assessment visit as a visit merely to begin the assessment process, which would then be ongoing, conducted both by the care worker and the organizer.
3 *Quality of life*. The concept of quality of life was fundamental to the project in that it acted as a benchmark against which care workers and management staff could base their judgement of a user's condition at home. This required care workers to develop the ability to recognize that the circumstances in which users found themselves were not inevitable, and to consider a wide range of alternatives.
4 *Promote accessibility*. Care workers themselves were recruited from a range of the ethnic communities in Sandwell, and were therefore critical in the recruitment of users. The majority of users were referred by the SSD, even if the finances used were from the Department of Health project purse. Nevertheless, considerable efforts were made to identify methods of advertising the service which would reach all potential users, and particularly those within the target population.
5 *Maximization of individual potential*. Care workers not only had to recognize

that the user's environment was not inevitable, but that their state of being, similarly, could be open to development. In this sense, the project could be said to have an educational or developmental objective. Users were not just to be helped, but to be supported in helping themselves. Even – or especially – those users with the most debilitating of conditions were expected to show some improvement in self-care and/or awareness. The emphasis upon this for the users led the staff to see that this applied equally to them. If staff are not continually learning and developing, neither will users.

This belief came to be fundamental to the training strategy of the project. Training came to mean three things, which were planned in a distinctive way but which, of course, overlapped. First was the concept of 'training towards organizational development'. This concentrated on the establishment and development of the organization by all who participated, to develop ownership and to ensure that the widest possible expertise was available in planning direction. Critical to this is a shared understanding of the accountability trail for the organization (see p. 30).

Organizational understanding and development was fed by 'training towards personal development'. Organizations will only change and develop and grow if the people within them are able to do so too. Thus the thrust of much of the training was developmental; that is, it assumed that people were able to participate in and contribute to organizational growth, and provided them with opportunities to explore their own role and performance within the project.

Third, the project provided 'training towards professional development', for management board, staff and care workers. Again, this assumed not just that performance would improve through better capability of staff, but that the project owed a duty to its staff to enable them to develop their professional competencies in whatever direction enabled appropriate development. This would, of course, in turn give staff greater confidence in contributing their own unique perceptions and abilities to the improvement of the service.

Following the initial training of the first tranche of staff, there would be few opportunities of working in such a way again. Later in the year, an induction and training strategy was devised which would ensure that all newly appointed staff were inducted into the organization in such a way as to give them the maximum information about the project, and an understanding of the ethos underlying its development (see Table 3.2).

Training groups were formed which would allow learning and support for new staff from their colleagues as well as management. The monthly meetings of training groups – the nearest one can get to staff meetings in an organization with such fluid working patterns – encourage the growth of collegiality, a commitment to the organization and offer an opportunity to raise issues of concern. As far as possible, the agenda is shared between management staff and care workers. A major item for the groups is to identify staff training needs, while a major item for management is to develop opportunities to explore the ethos of the organization. The training groups became a significant forum for implementation of the action

Table 3.2 Victoria Visiting Venture: Induction and training programme

1 *Interview.* All new entrants to the staff are given an induction interview by the project organizer or coordinator, which includes:

- a brief history of the project
- an account of the project's funding
- exploration of the individual's skills
- a review of training possibilities to deal with any deficiencies
- an account of training resources, including NVQ and in-house training
- the project's accountability trail
- a review of pay and conditions of employment
- a review of health and safety issues
- an introduction to the ethos and philosophy of the project

2 *Brochure.* All new entrants receive a copy of the project brochure, and are given an opportunity to discuss, and ask questions about, it. The brochure includes:

- the project mission statement
- the statement of equal opportunities
- a statement of needs-led provision
- the project management objectives
- an account of the project's reporting, evaluation and monitoring processes
- a statement of the induction, training and appraisal policy
- case studies of the care programmes provided by the project
- a statement of the eligibility criteria
- the users' appeals procedure

3 *Supervision*

- new care workers will be paired with existing staff, acting as mentors, for a period appropriate to their experience
- a review of the worker's performance will be conducted by the coordinator or organizer, including discussions with the users and mentors, before individual visits are assigned
- early assignments will normally be on a short-term basis, and will be evaluated

4 *Training groups*

- all workers are allocated to a training group
- groups will comprise six or seven workers structured to combine diversity of experience, length of service, age, gender and ethnicity
- training groups meet monthly, and follow a combination of the agenda set by management and their own agenda; the training groups address issues of concern to themselves and to the project, share individual problems and successes, and identify training needs for themselves and for all care workers

plans arising out of the application for recognition of Victoria Visiting Venture as an Investor in People.

People or systems?

Often, the main focus in change is on the systems employed by an organization. But change is above all about people, about their capacity for, and their ability to accept, change. The way that people in an organization treat each other is possibly the single most influential factor in determining the success or failure of an organization in change. This in turn can be influenced by, and is symbolized by, the procedures and systems which the organization has in place, and how it implements them. But the people come first.

PLANNING FOR GROWTH

Strategic planning

A strategic plan offers a vision of the sort of service which the organization wants to deliver, and therefore of the sort of organization needed to deliver it. It offers:

- A clear statement of aims and objectives: this is both high-flown, an opportunity to fantasize, coupled with the need to set specific practical targets.
- A structure in which decisions can be made: this gives staff in day-to-day management and direct service delivery a context to which they can refer. This requires the plan to be rooted in hard practicalities.
- An opportunity for all management committee members and staff to participate in policy-making: this directs the committee to its primary task, and away from staff tasks.
- A calendar of regular activities: the planning cycle gives a committee direction and purpose, while remaining sufficiently flexible to incorporate unforeseen issues.
- An action plan, with a timetable and responsible persons: this allows the committee to discharge its function of setting targets, monitoring and evaluating, and gives all members a clear and achievable individual aim.
- Clear guidelines for the committee: a plan keeps the committee on task.
- The committee's priorities: allowing the committee to allocate resources (i.e. money, time and personnel) appropriately.
- A vision for the future: giving the committee and staff practical goals and dreams.

A strategic plan does not have to be – indeed, is better for not being – a large and complex document. It should be, at least in one of its forms, a

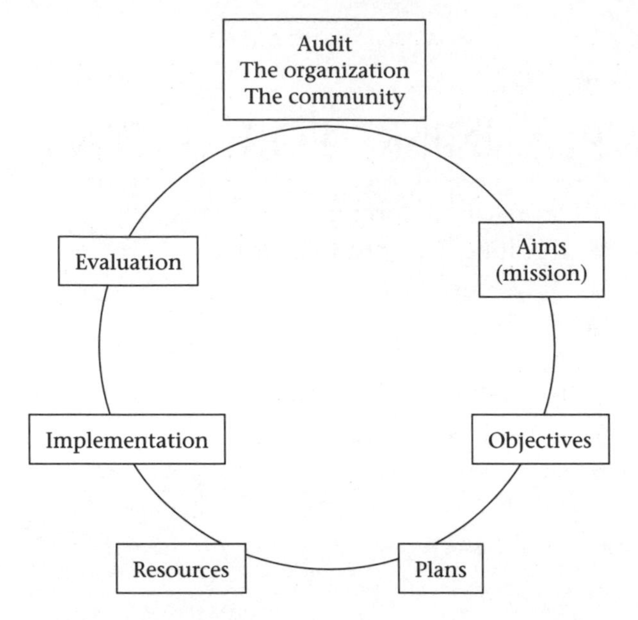

Figure 4.1 The strategic planning cycle

simple two- or three-page statement that is accessible to staff, users, potential funders and the general public. But it, together with its detailed supplements, and appendices comprising budgets, policies and procedures, will provide a comprehensive profile of the organization. A typical annual planning cycle is shown in Fig. 4.1.

The audit

Organizations are becoming accustomed to the idea of regularly spending some time in reviewing their current situation. The use of the term in a social or organizational sense gained currency following the Church of England 'Faith in the City' report, which recommended that each parish record the resources available within its boundaries. An organization with a brief to develop community resources might assess and record the elements listed in Table 4.1. The compilation of such data may be a massive undertaking, but it is likely that most of this information will be accessible. This is an exercise which, initially, may take a substantial amount of time. But if performed first within the committee and staff group, it will reveal the amount of local information held within the organization. A more detailed audit can then be conducted by a working party of the committee over a longer period of time (see, for example, Hawtin *et al.* 1994). This should then be updated annually, with full audits held every, say, four or five years. The community audit is one aspect of the organizational audit: the information and knowledge about the community which the organization has at its disposal.

An organizational audit will also comprise an inventory of other accessible

Table 4.1 Elements of a community audit

Education: schools, Adult education centres, colleges, Pre-school/under-5 facilities, supplementary schools
Places of worship: mosques, churches, chapels, temples, synagogues
Health: surgeries, clinics, hospitals
Transport: bus services, train services, taxi companies, accessible places
Entertainments: cinemas, theatres, bowling alleys, leisure centres, music halls/pubs
Sports: clubs, venues
Food and drink: pubs, cafes, restaurants, wine bars
Meeting places: open-air, under cover, youth activities, clubs, meeting places, playgrounds
Recreational spaces: parks, sports grounds, playgrounds
Voluntary organizations: community organizations, organizations for personal support, health and community care
Key figures: official community leaders, unofficial community leaders, opportunities for community leadership, opportunities for community participation
Trading: shops, marketplaces
Housing: types of accommodation, facilities for the elderly, facilities for those with disabilities, facilities for the homeless
Employment: employment figures, employment opportunities, facilities for the part and full unemployed
Demography: age, ethnic origin, lone parents, registers of poverty
Communications: local newspapers, free newspapers, news sheets
Safety: crime figures, crime patterns
Image: perceptions of the community by residents, perceptions of the community by non-residents

resources. These are likely to fall under the headings of personnel time, skills, knowledge and expertise; physical resources (premises and equipment); and less tangible features such as time available and reputation. This may not just be a list of the things which the organization possesses, but rather of those things to which the organization has access. It will be followed by a list of those things which the organization *doesn't* have access to, and which it wants or needs. A familiar procedure for an audit is through the compilation of a SWOT (strengths, weaknesses, opportunities and threats) chart. While practised seminar participants may groan at the prospect of yet another SWOT exercise, it is still one of the most effective ways of getting groups to consider their organizational assets – and defects – in an objective way.

There are numerous methods by which organization members can be distanced from their roles in order to shape an objective view. One project found that writing its premature obituary allowed members to consider what they wished to achieve. A series of statements made by the group of care workers, managers and committee members about a year after the project's inception was prioritized as follows:

We've helped people do things they didn't think they could do.
We're satisfied with our work so far.
We've taken risks.
We've brought different ethnic groups together.
The Department of Health and social services department have asked us to extend the project.
We've made some carers' lives much easier.
We've raised the project's profile.
We've given people what they really wanted.
We've kept people out of residential care.
Some of our care workers are difficult.
The project has received national recognition.
It's got better every year.
We've made some mistakes.
We've done better than social services.
We've shown the importance of the voluntary sector.
We've spent up to budget every year.
We all get on OK.

The aims

We saw in Chapter 3 a way in which a mission statement, or statement of aims, can be compiled within a management group. Such a statement will normally be at the heart of organizational practice. Handy (1988: 127), for example, writes:

> Most organizations have or should have: A cause, a vision or an overriding purpose, one which is long on rhetoric and short on numbers. That is fine, since its purpose is to inspire rather than to direct activity. But if anything is to happen, the cause must be supported by:
>
> - A set of specific tasks or areas of specific activity to be tackled in support of that cause.
> - And a set of measures which will indicate what success means in each task.

The mission statement itself will rarely need to be altered, although a committee will at least consider its meaning and application every year, perhaps at or around the time of the annual general meeting. It is also important that the statement is understood and affirmed by all members of the group, especially new members of committee and staff. The committee will need to consider whether internal or external pressures have arisen that demand some change in emphasis in the statement, and will certainly need to review the extent to which the organization has adhered to the statement during the past year. This may lead to some reconsideration of practice.

Developing organizational objectives

Following the agreement on aims, the group needs to analyse how this can be translated into a set of observable, and where possible measurable, objectives. These may be of two distinct types. The first will be concerned with the delivery of, and development of, the service which the organization provides. The second set of objectives will be concerned with the business aspects of the organization, and will be looked at in Chapter 5. The committee and staff of one voluntary organization agreed a set of service objectives which arose directly out of the mission statement, and attached to each objective a set of standards to be used in monitoring and evaluation:

1. *To maintain an innovative thinking environment which will empower clients by a process of continuous assessment*: by continuous assessment of the provision; regular care worker meetings and group supervision; management committee and staff training and development workshops; external evaluation of the service; a complaints procedure; exploration of relationships between care workers and service users; appraisal; and access for care workers to the management of the organization.
2. *To ensure equal access to a culturally sensitive service, especially by people who are under-represented in the delivery of the project's services*: by collection of statistics of the client group and the target area; statistics of workers; accessibility of information; and networking with other organizations and agencies.
3. *To provide an efficient and accessible system of administration which enables clients to get what they need; and care workers to do their job as effectively as possible*: by promoting accessibility of language; responsiveness; accuracy of information; confidentiality; and minimising administration.
4. *To maintain and display an assertive and professional management style; to provide systems which effectively allocate personnel and resources. The project coordinator and organizer will present themselves and the organization as a professional service to the community*: by the appearance of the office; the appearance of staff; financial controls; care of staff (controlling hours, pay, terms and conditions of employment, appeals, etc.); following approved procedures and criteria for prioritization; staff training; consistent application of principles and behaviour; calculation of actual unit costs of the service; matching of staff and clients; cost-effectiveness.
5. *To support all project staff by a comprehensive training programme and an open and facilitative consultation process*: through training, appraisal, staff support, evaluation, staff participation in decision-making, and care worker representation in management.

Objectives need:

- to arise out of the aims or mission statement;
- to cover all the parts of the organization that provide or contribute to the service;

- to be clear;
- to be susceptible to monitoring and evaluation.

Planning

Preparing plans to achieve the objectives of the service is the fourth key function of the management group, and may be the most neglected. It comprises a list of steps which will lead to the desired output. It first of all involves identifying the key issues for the planning period arising from a review of the objectives. An example is given in Table 4.2.

Once the key issues have been identified, each will have an action plan attached to it, with steps to be taken to achieve each goal. (Action plans will be considered in more detail in Chapter 5.) In some areas, the goals are quite vague, because it is normally inappropriate for a full committee to consider detail. In this case, each issue or goal will be allocated to individual members of committee or staff for the detail to be filled out and brought back for committee approval. At this point, there will be formal appointment of responsible individuals or working parties, whose task will be to monitor the activities and report back on a regular basis.

Resources

Each individual plan will identify the resources – time, money, personnel and equipment – that are estimated to be needed to achieve the goal. The organization, and the key people responsible, whether staff or committee members, will need to commit themselves to this input. This is a useful exercise in itself to give volunteers a sense of purpose and, ultimately, achievement. Such commitments also allow volunteers to gauge the time and effort they are prepared to put at the organization's disposal over the coming year. Each plan will have a time chart attached to allow monitoring to take place.

Implementation

The implementation of strategic plans will not necessarily be among the duties of a volunteer management committee, although there may be individuals who can be appropriately matched to specific goals. The task of the management committee is to monitor implementation; that is, to ensure that what has been planned to happen at or by a specific time has happened. Where it has not, the monitoring group will be responsible for reallocating time or personnel, amending the plan and reporting to committee. Monitoring need not be a highly specialized task, although where it applies to a whole organization, or the entire service delivered by an organization, it is a job often put out to an external consultancy. This perhaps says more about the need for management committees to identify their own key tasks than about the complexity of the task.

Table 4.2 Sample planning document for 1995–97

1 *Management committee/board of directors*
- Implement functions agreed in the previous year
- Recruit company secretary
- Recruit 'entrepreneurial' members
- Define the role of the board in developing policy and laying down principles

2 *Quality*
- Maintaining appraisals, training, in-house training
- Marketing; defining our purpose as a specialist quality service
- Benchmarking
- Monitoring and evaluation
- Supervision
- Innovation in the needs-led element of service (e.g. target groups: some mental health groups, some ethnic groups) (N.B. lottery money)

3 *Policies and procedures*
- Review all policies and procedures in committee
- Better contracts of employment (re: employment law, full-time staff and sessional staff)

4 *Post-entrepreneurial issues*
- Develop networking and shared facilities
- Provide, market and sell training
- Consider full-time staff support roles, develop competencies
- Develop TEC training offers
- Develop board competencies

5 *Networking, cooperation and federation*
- Develop board role
- Develop university and other regional relationships
- Sew together the patchwork of provision (e.g. providers' forum, training programmes)

6 *Finance*
- Develop private care provision
- Monitor and control finances, income and expenditure
- Develop staff skills in financial supervision
- Monitor SSD contract

7 *Office Accommodation*
- Develop a strategy

Evaluation

While monitoring is concerned with determining whether, and to what extent, a desired action is being or has been performed, evaluation is concerned with the worth of the action: Has the action achieved the overall objective quoted in the plan? And does the objective contribute to the aims of the organization as the committee originally envisaged it would? The collection of material to help achieve this critical evaluative role can probably be better performed by someone with an objective viewpoint, who can be, and is seen as, detached from the delivery of the service. But monitoring and evaluation cannot take place without the detailed planning and setting of goals that is the task of management; and, ultimately, it is the committee's job to evaluate the work of the evaluator.

The importance of policies and procedures

It can be seen from this approach to strategic planning that the role of the management committee can be structured in order to achieve clear and specific tasks which will shape the organization in order to deliver the central service or services. Some of this work will involve setting up procedures to which the organization will ordinarily work. These procedures will define the organization's relationship with its users, with its funders and with its staff. Procedures, which will be negotiated with teams often comprising representatives of users and staff, allow an organization's practices to be predictable and consistent. Procedures will best be produced when there is a perceived need for them, rather than as a token process.

The following three sample policies/procedures will be discussed in turn: a complaints procedure, health and safety policy, and criteria for eligibility.

Complaints procedure

A complaints procedure will comprise a policy statement by the organization outlining its belief about the place complaints may have in the development of a quality service, followed by a procedure addressed to users:

Introduction

The Citizen's Charter sets out the key principles of public service, namely that people are entitled to expect:

- explicit *standards* for the services they use;
- access to full, accurate *information* about services and how they are performing;
- their *voices* to be heard so that they have a say in how services are provided and a *choice* wherever possible;
- services to be provided by *courteous and helpful* staff;
- simple and effective *complaints* procedures;
- real *value for money*.

(Department of Health 1994)

We support this approach to the provision of services. The standards for dealing with complaints have been drafted in the same document. They are:

- well publicized and readily accessible complaints procedures;
- complaints to be dealt with fairly, openly and without delay;
- specific time-scales for handling different stages of the complaints procedure;
- complaints covering more than one agency to be handled in a coordinated way which minimizes inconvenience for the complainant;
- information to be available on how people can make complaints to the Local Government Ombudsman and Health Services Commissioner.

We recognize that our service will not always achieve the quality required by the service standards. We therefore make a commitment to a continuous monitoring of its service, and to seeking out instances where the service fails to reach the agreed standards.

To users:

You can use this procedure when:

- An assessment visit does not happen at the time stated, or the result of the assessment visit is late, or does not reflect sufficiently the needs of the user.
- Adjustments are not made to the assessment as and when needed.
- The care worker allocated is not able to meet the user's needs in accordance with the assessment, or does not conform to the Code of Practice.

If you wish to complain about a refusal to accept a referral, or the withdrawing of part or all of the service, a separate procedure is in place. The project coordinator or project organizer can advise you on what you need to do.

How do I make my complaint?

First, discuss your complaint with your care worker. It may be that the problem can be solved between the two of you.

If the concern you have is not solved, or if for any reason you do not want to discuss it with your care worker, contact the project coordinator or project organizer. One of them will visit you within 3 days in order to discuss your complaint and come up with a solution.

If you are still not happy with the service you are receiving, you can complain directly to the management committee. You should do this in writing, and address it to the chairperson. Within 14 days, the committee will invite you to present your case personally, accompanied by a friend, an interpreter or someone who will put your complaint for you. Your case will be heard by a panel of about three committee members.

All complaints will be looked at fully, fairly and carefully. Urgent complaints are given priority. You will be kept informed of what is happening during and at the end of each stage. The committee will give you their decision in writing. You can also complain to the borough council if:

- you are not happy with the Committee's decision, or
- your complaint is with the social services department.

Health and safety policy

The health and safety policy is primarily a structure for the protection of staff. Again, it comprises a statement of policy and intent, followed by a procedure:

Statement of policy and intent

1 The management committee considers that one of its primary objectives is the achievement and maintenance of a high standard of health and safety for all its employees and volunteers.
2 They also recognize and accept their corporate responsibility to provide a healthy and safe working environment for all their employees and volunteers, and for users, carers and other members of the public concerned with the organization.
3 The management committee will take all reasonable steps to fulfil this responsibility and will pay particular attention to meeting the requirements of the Health and Safety at Work, etc. Act 1974, and all relevant statutory provisions.
4 The committee requires management to display a positive attitude towards health and safety.
5 The committee requires employees at all levels to pursue their objectives in respect of health and safety.

The organization

The duties of the project coordinator/manager are:

1 To pursue the objectives of the management committee in respect of health and safety.
2 To set up arrangements in the organization to cover all health and safety requirements, to produce a written statement of those arrangements, and to bring it, and Parts 1 and 2 of the committee's statement, to the attention of all staff. The statement is to be revised and republished as necessary. To monitor effectively the implementation of the arrangements.
3 To be available to any member of staff or volunteer to discuss and to seek to resolve health and safety problems not solved at another level.
4 To report to the committee those instances where the coordinator/ manager's authority does not allow the elimination or reduction to a

satisfactory level of a hazard, but to take all necessary short-term measures to avoid danger pending rectification.

5 To ensure that a system is established for the reporting, recording and investigation of accidents, and that all reasonable steps are taken to prevent recurrences.
6 To ensure that health and safety matters are raised as an item on the agenda of training group meetings, and that all employees are alerted, where appropriate through the groups, to any issues concerning them.
7 To ensure that new employees are briefed about safety arrangements; in particular, to ensure they are given a copy of the organization's statement and the opportunity to read it before starting work.
8 To ensure that effective arrangements are in force to facilitate ready evacuation of the buildings in case of fire or other emergency, and that fire-fighting equipment is available and maintained.

Monitoring

1 The management committee will monitor safety performance and set targets as necessary. It will review on an annual basis accidents reported by employees and volunteers of the organization.
2 The project coordinator/manager will monitor the health and safety aspects of the work performed by the employees and volunteers of the organization, and take such steps as are necessary to:
   - secure adequate training for them;
   - provide personal protective equipment where appropriate;
   - ensure that all procedures undertaken by the staff have been subjected to an assessment of the risks involved.

Organization for safety

1 It is the responsibility of the *project coordinator* to:
   - take day-to-day responsibility for all health and safety matters in the organization;
   - liaise with the management committee on policy issues;
   - ensure that the policy is activated;
   - ensure that problems in implementing the health and safety policy are reported to the committee;
   - draw up procedures and review them annually;
   - arrange for staff to be informed and trained;
   - check that procedures are followed in the offices;
   - identify any hazard and estimate the extent of the risk involved to an employee or volunteer working in the home of a user of the project.
2 It is the responsibility of the *project organizer* to:
   - check that procedures are followed when employees are on duty in other people's homes;
   - act on reports from staff within an agreed time-scale and report problems;
   - assist the project coordinator/manager in the training of staff.

3 It is the responsibility of *all employees and volunteers* to:
- check that the site of their work is safe;
- check equipment is safe before it is used;
- ensure that safe procedures are followed;
- ensure that protective equipment is used;
- report any problems to the project organizer or project coordinator;
- raise any training needs with the project coordinator.

Hazardous practices and conditions

1 The project organizer and/or project coordinator/manager will draw to the attention of all staff the hazards involved in:
- lifting, supporting, washing and other physical contact with users;
- cleaning, cooking, conducting repairs and other domestic tasks;
- using electrical and gas-fired equipment;
- any specific tasks required by the user and included in the assessment.

2 The assessment of a user will include reference to any health and safety hazards in addition to the day-to-day hazards listed above. Such hazards will be drawn to the attention of the allocated care worker(s) in writing before their first unaccompanied visit.

Criteria for eligibility

The development of criteria for eligibility for the service, or access criteria, is a more complex task than the drafting of a complaints procedure or a health and safety policy. It is vital that the organization's mission statement is used as the foundation upon which access criteria are developed, and that the committee and staff are directly involved in their formulation, in, for instance, a full-day workshop. A sample policy might be based upon the document *Inspecting Home Care Services* (DHSS 1990), comprising once again a statement of intent, followed by a detailed categorization of levels of dependence and the elements of users' status and environment which would be taken into consideration in staff prioritization of need.

Introductory statement

We affirm that everyone is entitled to privacy, dignity, independence, choice, rights and fulfilment.

This document specifies the criteria to be taken into account in determining the eligibility of a potential client to receive the service. Where the pressure on the service is such that judgements need to be made in the prioritization of clients, the criteria will be used in considering the acceptance of new clients.

1 Levels of dependence

The following categories will apply to all clients:

High: large degree of physical/mental impairment. Needs help with everyday tasks such as feeding, dressing and toileting. Very poor mobility. Dementia or behaviour which suggests a need for almost constant supervision for their own safety.
Medium: some physical/mental impairment or frailty. May be confused. Not dependent for everyday tasks but not entirely self-caring.
Low: able to be self-caring. Physically well, mentally alert.
Clients with a high level of dependence will be given priority.

2 The following criteria are judged to be significant in the assessment of users' eligibility to receive the service:

User's status and environment

Criteria	*Relevance/priority*
Gender	None
Age	60+ years
Type of household	The isolated always have priority
Marital status	Recent loss of partner
Whereabouts of spouse/partner	Recent hospitalization of partner
Ethnic group	Afro-Caribbean and Asian priority
Housing tenure	None
Accommodation type	Housing condition will be considered
Sheltered housing	Degree of shelter will have influence
Alarm system	None
Telephone	None
Source of referral	Self-referrals have priority
Circumstances of referral	Emergencies, but not crisis service

Assessment
Levels of dependence in the following categories will be taken into account: mobility, sight, hearing, memory, confusion, anxiety, depression, incontinence, catheter/colostomy, abilities, abuse (presence of abuse may delay withdrawal), social network, medication (N.B. medication will not be administered by the service). The potential of the client to show improvement to the extent of eventual withdrawal of the service on the grounds of no further need may be taken into account as grounds for acceptance.

Service considerations
The receipt of these services will not be taken into account: mobile meals, community nurse, bathing attendant, laundry service, care attendant/sitting, social/lunch club, day centre, day hospital, volunteer

visitor, private domestic help, private nursing care, social worker, occupational therapist, health visitor, chiropodist, etc. The absence of appropriate aids/adaptations may constitute grounds for refusal of a client.

Other care
The availability of care elsewhere will be taken into account in the refusal of a client, where it is more, equally or less appropriate than that offered by the service.

3 Appeals

3.1 Assessment will normally be conducted by the project coordinator and project organizer. In the event of a refusal to accept the client, he or she, his or her carer(s), or other representative may appeal.
3.2 The appeal will be heard within 14 days of receipt of the appeal by a panel comprising three members of the management committee. No member of the panel shall have an interest in the client beyond that of a potential service provider.
3.3 The applicant or his or her representative will present the case for acceptance to the panel. The panel may question the applicant. The project coordinator or project organizer may question the applicant.
3.4 The project coordinator or project organizer will present the reasons for refusal. The panel may question. The applicant may question.
3.5 The applicant may sum up his or her case.
3.6 The project coordinator or project organizer may sum up his or her case.
3.7 The panel will withdraw to consider its decision. The decision will be notified to the applicant and to the project coordinator or project organizer as soon as possible and, in any case, in writing to both within 3 days.

Planning systems for growth

We have seen in Chapter 3 that organizations are primarily about people. But growing organizations have an organic life of their own, which will be represented by the systems – the policies and procedures – by which they operate. Just as we judge individuals by their behaviour, so we assess organizations by what they do; and a healthy organization is one that demonstrates a consistency of behaviour that allows us to 'get a handle' on it. The systems are the 'outward and visible' manifestations of the inner, invisible values.

THE MANAGEMENT OF VOLUNTARY ORGANIZATIONS

- ▲ Ethical management
- ▲ Participation
- ▲ Tasks of management
- ▲ Skills of management
- ▲ Values of management
- ▲ Leadership
- ▲ Power
- ▲ Financial management
- ▲ The needs of voluntary organizations

How will a voluntary organization define its own needs in preparing for a period of change?

The needs of voluntary organizations

It has been claimed, here and elsewhere, that voluntary organizations are different from the private and public sector in that they are more likely to be value-led. It has been suggested above that this difference may not be as stark as some claim it to be. It is certainly more likely to be useful for voluntary staff to consider the similarities, rather than the differences, they have with other sectors. This will encourage such exercises as benchmarking, where indispensable lessons can be learnt from elsewhere.

It may be, as perhaps would be claimed by those working in the voluntary sector, that voluntary organizations are more humane than businesses, and more human than the public sector. In any event, we may start from the premise that voluntary organizations, like people, have needs. Identifying these needs may provide an insight into the potential that the voluntary sector has to change.

Voluntary organizations of any age, like people, need a set of *values* by which to conduct their lives. It is these values – effectively or otherwise summed up in a mission statement or statement of aims – which underlie the conduct of the organization. These values have to be represented in every document issued, every policy and procedure followed, every part of every service delivered. There therefore needs to be a structured system by which these values are communicated to new workers and new users. The ethical basis of the voluntary sector is generally accepted. It is often referred to as an incentive by workers, particularly when comparing their work to the private sector, often as a reasonable substitute for less favourable terms and conditions of work. But it is also often heard as an excuse for sloppy practices, and an absence of systematic methods of work.

An ethical approach to the management of a voluntary organization is critical to its sustained success

The history of the development of management theory, since its beginnings as a discrete study in the early part of the twentieth century, is of a development from a theory of scientific management ('In the past, the man has been first; in the future, the system must be first': Taylor 1911) to an approach based upon the nature of human relations. Management may be an art rather than a science, in the traditional understanding. It requires leaps of the imagination accompanied by human empathy, followed by the exercise of a craft or technique.

What makes the structure of the public and voluntary sectors (and the halfway houses of Next Steps agencies) distinctive are the management role of non-professionals, and the moves towards user participation in management. And the dominant question is, 'Why don't people participate more?' This appeal is heard through all the structures and levels of public service, embracing the shortage of 'suitable' candidates, and the poor turnout of the electorate, for local government; the erratic responses to protest movements (such that when such movements do succeed in turning out large numbers on the streets, such as the Poll Tax protests and the actions against live animal exports of the early 1990s, the public response is one of surprise that the phlegmatic British ever take to the streets about anything); and the difficulty in recruiting to public offices such as school governorships.

Schumpeter's (1942) theory of representative democracy rested upon the assumption that the mass of the population would be alienated and apathetic; thus the current form of government is a response to human nature. It is possible, however, that the cause and effect are inverted here. It suits the rulers of society at all levels to advocate a system of representative democracy, which encourages – in fact demands – the minimum of participation between elections. In all the great purposes of statehood – in the development of education, health care, the public infrastructure – the role of the public has always been secondary, as passive recipients. Only through the consumer movements of the 1980s has the public been invited to comment upon, and respond to, the effectiveness of public service; and the thrust has been very much towards accountability through choice, rather than through participation.

However much we complain about the apathy of the public – of parents, of patients, of consumers – it is clearly more convenient for those of us who run things that the current levels of participation remain as they are. Hence, when opportunities arise – health authority public meetings, school governors' meetings – we are happier to bemoan the apathy of the parents whose fault it is in not turning up to take an active part in their children's education, than to ask how, after 150 years of top-down management, we can begin to try to build the confidence of the public, that their ideas and needs will not continue to be treated with the contempt, however benevolently presented, of the professional and of the politician. We see what we wish to see, as did Tony Crosland (1956):

> Experience shows that only a small minority of the population wish to participate . . . the majority prefer to lead a full family life and to cultivate their gardens and a good thing too. We do not necessarily want a busy, bustling society in which everyone is politically active and fussing around in an interfering and responsible manner and herding us all into participatory groups. The threat to privacy and freedom would be intolerable.

The fact is that we have to accept that it is *our* fault when people don't turn up, don't apply, don't stand for election, and *our* responsibility to do something about it. The first step towards an ethical organization, as with a human being, is to begin to take the responsibility of failure on ourselves, and to be prepared to share decision-making with those whom it most affects. The absolute necessity of helping people to grow into participatory democracy was observed by John Stuart Mill (1952) in 1859: 'We do not learn to read or write, to ride or swim, by being merely told how to do it, but by doing it, so it is only by practising popular government on a limited scale, that the people will ever learn how to exercise it on a larger scale'; and repeated more recently by Michael Duane (1991): 'Democracy, like language, needs practice from infancy if it is to become as much part of our natures as language is'. The development of participation, therefore, becomes more than a utilitarian aspiration, more than an ethical framework, but part of the life-blood of a mature society:

> It lies with all to superintend home life and state affairs alike, while despite our varied concerns we keep an adequate acquaintance with politics. We alone regard the man who takes no part in it, not as unobtrusive, but as useless, and we all at least give much thought to an action . . . we do not win friendship from benefit received, but from service rendered . . . In short, I declare that our whole city of Athens is an education for Greece.
>
> (Thucydides, Pericles' Funeral Speech)

It is possible to see in many workplaces the traditional trappings of a feudal state: an insistence upon stability and routine, together with the resistance to change which will be discussed below; a reliance upon homage and deference as a means of getting things done; a lack of mobility leading to fixed mind-sets; an emphasis upon (often unearned) status. It is precisely these characteristics that bring about the problems of the workplace which are being addressed today: sexual harassment, bullying, the need for assertiveness. These are symptoms of workplace structures that are unlikely to disappear until the structures themselves are changed. What we are left with is a style of leadership that, in the words of the social analyst Studs Terkel writing of a style of US government, can give people permission 'to be their own worst selves' (interview reported in the *Guardian*, 9 May 1992). Or, of course, their best selves. Terkel reminds us elsewhere just how awful the workplace can be:

> Work is by its very nature about violence – to the spirit as well as to the body. It is about ulcers as well as accidents, about shouting matches as well as fistfights, about nervous breakdowns as well as kicking the dog around. It is, above all (or beneath all) about daily humiliations. To survive the day is triumph enough for the walking wounded among the great many of us.
>
> (Terkel 1972: xiii)

The great justification for the dehumanizing workplace – and the dehumanizer's most effective weapon – is bureaucracy. The feudalist workplace uses bureaucratic systems to protect itself from challenge and change. Yet many of the systems now favoured to ensure protection for clients and workforces seem to be extremely bureaucratic: equal opportunity policies, health and safety procedures, codes of conduct, all add to the structures and to the paperwork, and therefore apparently to the restrictions upon freedom of the individual. A distinction has to be made between those systems which are designed to restrict the freedom of the worker, and those which are designed to enhance the freedom of all the individuals with a stake in the organization. So the question always has to be answered: 'For whose benefit is this procedure designed?' If the only answer is 'management', that is bureaucracy. The point is that bureaucratic systems dehumanize, while ethical systems are human-centred. At the heart of issues such as bureaucratization 'lies the question of our faith in human nature and its potential, and the amount of external or internal control needed for decision and action to be good and just' (Schubert 1990).

Maslow's well-known hierarchy of needs suggests that, once the primary physiological needs for sustenance, shelter and safety are met, the need for companionship and friendship is followed by the need for status and the respect of others, and the need for self-development and growth. This has a clear lesson for any organization. Herzberg develops this. For him, the chief factors leading to extreme job satisfaction, are:

> Achievement – self-fulfilment and personal growth by acquiring a new skill or bringing some project to fruition . . . ; Recognition – praise, promotion, a special reward or more money . . . ; Responsibility – some people respond to being responsible for a task; for planning without close supervision, for managing the performance of others, for being the leader. Effective delegation will be a motivator in these cases; The work

itself – some people work well because their task is intrinsically interesting to them.

(Herzberg 1966)

The antidote to bureaucracy is a set of rules that the workers make for themselves, and regularly review and recommit themselves to, and that grow out of the needs of the primary function of the organization and of the people that perform it; rules that allow flexibility and encourage initiative; rules that are codes and avoid ritualism. Kanter (1983) provides a checklist for managers of the bureaucratic nightmare:

1 Regard any new idea from below with suspicion – because it is new, and because it is from below.
2 Insist that people who need your approval to act first go through several other levels of management to get their signature.
3 Ask departments or individuals to challenge and criticize each others' proposals. (That saves you the job of deciding: you just pick the survivor.)
4 Express your criticisms freely, and withhold your praise. (That keeps people on their toes.) Let them know they can be fired at any time.
5 Treat problems as signs of failure, to discourage people from letting you know when something in their area isn't working.
6 Control everything carefully, make sure people count anything that can be counted, frequently.
7 Make decisions to reorganize or change policies in secret, and spring them on people unexpectedly. (That also keeps people on their toes.)
8 Make sure that any request for information is fully justified and that it isn't distributed too freely. (You don't want data to fall into the wrong hands.)
9 Assign lower-level managers, in the name of delegation and participation, responsibility for figuring out how to cut back, lay off or move people around.
10 Above all, never forget that you, the higher-ups, already know everything important about this business.

What, then, is the nature of effective ethical management within the voluntary sector? A series of interviews conducted with managers of local development agencies suggests that effective management:

- is supportive;
- continually uses the aims and objectives of the organization to define its direction;
- encourages change, experimentation and innovation;
- is people-centred, encouraging individual growth and development;
- is non-directive;
- holds the team together;
- understands and advances quality;
- monitors and evaluates;
- communicates;

- performs technical tasks (such as discharging financial and legal responsibilities) efficiently.

There was general agreement among these very experienced managers that such management skills are transferable. The activity to be managed comes first. The main purpose of management is to service it, enable it, empower it. But management also has its own expertise and specialisms, and it has a guidance function. It is in this last function that problems arise when the professional background of a manager is discounted. Managers do need to understand, if not to wholly encompass, the experience of direct service provision, and this understanding is repaid with the confidence of the workers.

In addition to a thoroughly worthy desire to stay in touch with their roots, voluntary sector managers may also suffer from some lack of self-esteem. There does seem to be an anti-management ethos within much of the voluntary sector, a feeling that the real work is done with the sleeves rolled up. Managers speak of not having a proper job if they sit at a desk. This goes in tandem with an anti-training ethos at many levels of the voluntary sector. Work in many parts of the sector may not seem like real work: it isn't routine; you can dress how you like; there are few hierarchies; the salaries are often hardly like real money; most of all, it's often enjoyable, which real work shouldn't be. Therefore, you shouldn't need to be trained to do it. Coupled with the shortage of organizational money ('How can I spend this money on me when there's so little for the clients?'), we can see why paid workers, let alone management committees, might resist training opportunities.

Ethical management is not so much a style of management as a management focus, one which centres upon personal growth. If you can look back with warmth to any manager you have worked with in your career, it is probable that what you recall is not so much 'how well you performed the task you were employed for', but what you gained, learned, enjoyed and felt rewarded about. It is likely that you also performed tasks pretty effectively.

Studying lists of the tasks of management compiled by the most popular management writers suggests activities such as planning, organizing, creating, motivating, directing, communicating, coordinating and controlling. What is missing? All but peripherally, the people who perform the key tasks in an organization are absent. Evaluating, appraising, developing and educating are key tasks of management that address the key issue – how to get the job done best. In 1993, the management staff and some members of the committee of one voluntary organization considered this standard list of tasks, and expanded it into a list of required skills, as shown in Table 5.1.

The left-handed organization

In studying this fairly random list as it emerged, it became clear to the participants that there seemed to be two different types of activity. One group, the right-hand column, seemed to be systemic, manipulative and with designated ends; the second group, the left-hand column, seemed to be person- and language-centred, with potentially open ends. At the time (and

Table 5.1 Management skills

Caring	Financial
Communicating	Political
Coordinating	Planning
Praising	Fund-raising
Analysing	Practical
Relating	Shaping
Reporting	Implementing
Innovating	Manual
Evaluating	Directing
Investigating	Organizing
Presenting	Controlling
Supporting	
Listening	
Negotiating	

in a predominantly female group), the columns were designated female and male respectively. Without making too much of this judgement, the right-hand group seemed to encompass skills and ways of doing things that were considered the arena of male expertise. They encompassed the perception of the new order for voluntary organizations – one where political, financial and planning skills are celebrated above personal, caring skills. This seemed especially to be the case in a local government culture which is dominated by men in senior policy-making and decision-making positions (this is not to suggest that the male characteristics are only and exclusively exercised by men and vice versa, just that it seemed a more male/female way of doing things). It was felt by the group that, while all the skills identified were necessary to complete the managerial task, the right-hand column seemed to dominate practice in the relationship between local government and health authority purchasers, and voluntary and private sector providers of community care. Yet there was no obvious reason why this should be so. The left-hand column skills seemed to be particularly exercised in the management of the voluntary sector, and seemed to be successful. There seemed to be no reason why the voluntary sector should be required to change its methods, yet its perception of the local authority was that it wanted to see such changes. This perception was strengthened by writings on the contract culture. While there was justifiable emphasis on the need to be business-like, there seemed to be no particular reason why the business-likeness had to take the form demanded by purchasers.

Herein lies a potential dilemma. Does a voluntary organization continue to collude in 'the game', changing its methods, its outlook and its style? Or does it identify the strengths it has – probably on the left-hand side of Table 5.1 – and insist on protecting these?

To take this simplistic classification a little further, this is not to argue that 'male-type' organizations cannot be ethical. But it does suggest that an ethical, people-centred, educational organization is likely to have, among its most prominent managerial skills, a strong representation of those skills in the left-hand column.

This analysis suggests that the ethical organization will be cautious and selective about the language it uses. Whereas the language of efficiency and roles will be prominent in the ends-oriented organization, fairness, justice, care, trust and responsibility will be key words in the ethical organization. It is therefore immediately evident why the voluntary sector is particularly well placed to operate in an ethical way, but equally obvious why it is now under pressure not to do so. Historically, some of the attributes ascribed to the voluntary sector – its idealism, its value-orientation, its reliance upon individual commitment and expression (manifested in the charismatic leader) – have been its weaknesses. The amateurism these qualities can lead to has been graphically documented (see, for example, Landry *et al.* 1985). If success can be attributed solely to the drive of one person, so can failure, as with the democratic accountability of the Merseyside Police Authority: Lady Simey, in giving evidence at an industrial tribunal, stated: 'Nobody could tell us what were the duties of a police authority. The chief constable told us our job was to pay up and shut up' (*Guardian*, 14 July 1992). So, also, in the world of the mental health charity: When a new chief executive discovered 'enough about the financial position to present management accounts to the charity's ruling council, he was told they were the first accounts the council had seen'. Until then, 'the only financial information given to the council had been verbal reports by the former director. She had allowed no other staff members to attend council meetings'. The relationship between the key paid staff and the accountable authority, in the form of board, committee or trust, has to be defined in terms of the ethical nature of the organization and of all its practices.

Above all, an ethical organization needs systems of moral and psychological support for its staff, its management (paid and voluntary) and its users: training, groupwork, appraisal, evaluation and access conducted in a non-judgemental way. It is not about creating such a strong organizational system that individuals have removed from them the necessity of making their own moral judgements. This will instead lead to the creation of a lowest common denominator of conduct based on rules. Rather, it will be represented in the centralization of the key worker in a strong collective purpose, and in the exploitation of the individual worker's own ethical purpose.

In addition to an explicit set of values and an identity, the ethical organization needs change. Change has been written about much recently as an ordeal to be survived. It is claimed that change deskills. It is presented as if it is a patch of oil on an otherwise clear road. We are all heading purposefully for our destination until we hit it. If we fail to manage the skid, we will slide off into the ditch. But steer carefully, allow for the new conditions, and we will come out the other side, able to continue our journey as if nothing much had happened. In reality, change is the road itself. Of course, individuals change all the time – if we do not change, we do not grow. Had the structures imposed by an industrial society not required routine and sameness, we would not have those expectations of our workplaces. Change must be built into the organization as one of its central purposes, to help to continuously develop its effectiveness. Drucker (1985) gives a number of examples of innovations which have changed our ways of solving human problems: purchase by instalment, the school textbook, the hospital, factory organization and the container industry. Handy (1988) adds the hospice movement, distance learning, takeaway food, sponsored runs and the garden centre, all ways in which social inventions have changed people's behaviour. Some industries have begun to develop a person-centred and growth-centred approach to personnel, through quality circles and through initiatives such as Ford's individual education/training budgets. In the field of community care, one North London project responded to the Department of Health's 'Caring for People Who Live at Home' project by developing an instant response by pager to the needs of older people living alone. While rarely needed, the application of new cheap technology to the model of sheltered housing (another innovation in itself) is an efficient and cost-effective answer to the rare but critical emergency call.

Change, therefore, is part of the way of life of an organization and is not imposed upon it. Change has indeed to be the fundamental purpose of the organization. Workers should be trained to expect, and to nurture, improvement. The development of an ethos of self-evaluation, of opportunities for growth, will lead to explicit commitments to staff as well as to users. For example: 'Everyone working with this organization, whether paid or volunteer, will, when they leave, be a more attractive proposition to other employers'. Thus the natural growth of the nurtured organization (as in Table 2.1) is mirrored by, and demands, the growth of all the individuals associated with it. This means that the same basic values applied to work with disadvantaged people should also be applicable to the organizations that work with them. The organization must accord the same rights to its staff as to its users; in particular, those defined by the Social Services Inspectorate (Social Services Inspectorate 1990) as privacy, independence, rights, dignity, choice and fulfilment.

These can be applied to the workplace just as they can to the residential home and to the domiciliary visiting service. The following are questions that might be asked by an ethical employer:

Privacy

- How does the workplace intrude into people's lives?
- Are employees allowed/encouraged to pursue their own interests in and beyond the workplace?
- Do employees' private lives enrich their work experience?
- Are there clearly defined boundaries between private and public lives?

Independence

- Are staff given opportunities for making decisions that affect their own jobs?
- Are staff given opportunities to participate in decision-making about the work of the organization?
- Are staff granted increasing autonomy as they gain experience?
- Are staff allowed to participate in the development of codes of conduct regarding their relationships with clients?

Rights

- Do staff have written terms and conditions of employment? Are these negotiated with staff and/or their representatives? Are they regularly reviewed?
- Is there a workable and effective system of appraisal?
- Do appraisal systems lead to an agreed programme of training and development?
- Are staff represented on the management committee/board?
- Is there an effective and utilized complaints procedure for staff?

Dignity

- Are all staff treated as of equal worth?
- Are staff consulted regularly on organizational policies?
- Are staff always treated as people with integrity?
- Is there an overriding belief that most of the time people do their best?
- Can staff feel that the actions of their managers are reliable, consistent and predictable?
- Are disciplinary procedures always confidential and conducted in private?
- Are there opportunities to discuss what they or others may perceive as instances of 'failure', and to recover from them?

Fulfilment

- Do staff leave the organization better qualified and/or prepared for a wider range of employment opportunities?
- Do staff have opportunities to discuss their ambitions and aspirations?
- Are staff offered regular opportunities to reflect on their role and achievements?
- Are successes publicly celebrated and failures privately analysed?

Choice

- Do staff have opportunities to make choices in their work; for example, some flexibility regarding clients, type of work, etc.?
- Do staff have the opportunity to reflect on their relationships within the workplace?
- Do staff have some flexibility over working arrangements?

These are the fundamental questions an organization's managers might ask themselves, and their staff, in evaluating the impact that the organization has on its workforce. From these, it is possible to identify the characteristics which an ethical organization is likely to exhibit (as we shall see, these will lead to the type of quality audit suggested in Chapter 6):

Productive behaviour of successful organizations

1. *Responsiveness*: the organization will respond quickly and appropriately to signs of difficulty or discontent, complaints and grievances.
2. *Attentiveness*: the organization will actively seek out the views and feelings of its staff, and will be sensitive to their moods and emotions.

3 *Development*: the organization will seek to change and grow alongside its staff, and will expect the staff to develop personally and professionally.
4 *Honesty*: the organization will seek at all times to be honest with staff, except where this is incompatible with appropriate individual confidentiality, about its own plans and procedures.
5 *Empathy*: the organization will seek at all times to view issues and problems from the point of view of the staff and, where possible and compatible with the interests of the clients, to share in their interests.
6 *Consistency*: the organization will follow accepted procedures, and behave in such a way that staff may reasonably predict the outcome of personal and professional interactions.
7 *Involvement*: the organization will encourage the staff to become involved at appropriate stages of the decision-making process at all its levels and in all its transactions.

Leadership (and participation in leadership)

The key characteristic of anyone in a leadership role, whether a relatively isolated manager or a member of a team, is the ability to identify the qualities that they themselves bring to the organization. Training for management concentrates rightly on skills and knowledge, but may neglect to emphasize the importance of self-awareness, which allows team-building to focus on developing a team with all-round strengths. It is particularly important for members of a management team to recognize their own qualities and those of others, and to value them. Such explicit identification can remove the obstacles to cooperative working that bedevil teams, which are often as much about personal incompatibilities as about an effective blending of skills. The work of Belbin (1981) implies that team members will by definition find it difficult to work with their colleagues, unless the essential differences in approach are openly acknowledged.

An exercise performed with four members of the management team of a small organization elicited the self-perceptions laid out in Fig. 5.1. The comparative emotional detachment identified in themselves by the assistant manager and the board officer might have become a source of irritation leading to a less than effective working partnership; its acknowledgement led to an appreciation of the value of differing viewpoints and of the need to combine the necessary but incompatible, the charismatic enthusiast with the objective evaluator, in viewing the work of the organization. The need for a similar distribution of skills and inclinations on a management committee has already been explored. Smaller management teams similarly need to encompass and to absorb the one who says 'Why', the one who says 'No', the one who says 'Hold it', the one who says 'Let's get on', the one who says 'We've got this wrong', and the one who says 'Haven't we done well', particularly so when one member may need to perform a number of these functions.

The characteristics listed by the participants in this exercise tend to concentrate on fairly traditional images of leadership. They focus on skills, knowledge

General manager

Commitment
Energy and enthusiasm
Knowledge
Humour
Stability
Leadership

Assistant manager

Ability to listen well
Ability to communicate well
Ability to be objective
Determination
Computation skills
Emotional detachment

Senior officer of board

Enthusiasm
Support
Objectiveness
Empowerment
Outside awareness of related issues
Skills around volunteering issues
Humour
Strong belief

Administration officer

Commitment
Caring about the organization
Progression
Extra time
Listening
Reliability

Figure 5.1 What do we bring?

and characteristics, rather than on practice. In modern voluntary organizations, there needs to be at least an equal emphasis on processes – the consistent practices followed in order to help employees to share in the ownership of the organization. This means, as is implied throughout this book, that a structure of consultation is essential, the key characteristics of which will be power (not just influence), servicing (not adoption), identifying need, accessibility and information.

Power

This model does imply some relaxation of control, although not of power, by management. As with public participation in the public and voluntary sectors, the development of participation by the workforce is slow to take off in the voluntary sector. This does not suggest that we should stop trying. It may take many years of constructive leadership by consultation to give participants the confidence to see that their views are respected and count. Tony Crosland's (1956) view is as false here as it is in the public domain. As Schattschneider (1960: 105) noted: 'It is profoundly characteristic that responsibility for widespread non-participation is attributed wholly to the ignorance, indifference and shiftlessness of the people'. While the dominant groups within society – in the workplace, in community organizations and among the public at large – can rely on such an attribution, the present order will remain unthreatened. Thus Lukes' (1974: 15) theory that the bases of power may be sufficiently strong to ensure that a 'mobilisation of bias' occurs which excludes certain powerless groups from the arena altogether.

In order to study patterns of participation and powerlessness, one has to study power 'at the point where its intention, if it has one, is completely invested in its real and effective practices' (Foucault 1976). As Gaventa (1980) has shown at the level of an entire economic and geographic community, quiescence can be so deeply ingrained by the absolute control of physical and cultural resources by the elite, that even a simple cost–benefit analysis of the potential outcomes of protest could never arise. The powerless community (or the workforce) internalizes the values and norms of the powerful to such effect that participation cannot appear on anyone's agenda.

In order to lay the foundations for a workplace where genuine participation in decision-making takes place, it has to operate as an underlying assumption in all processes. Power is not a finite commodity, like a cake to be sliced up – the more you get, the less they get. The power of the leader (except perhaps that power which operates outside of a moral framework, and therefore does not concern us here) does not diminish when it is shared. Conversely, it can be said that real influence by consent increases when decision-making structures are opened up and opened out. Structures which allow such participation need to be allowed to grow at all levels of the workplace, and eventually confidence in them will develop, and people will value them, use them and at last take them for granted.

Servicing

The structures which permit participation must be open to perpetual scrutiny. They therefore have to be serviced, as they can be complex and, without care, excessively time-consuming. But the servicing structures, such as professional advice, must not adopt (i.e. take over in order to dominate) the processes, for reasons of 'efficiency'.

Identifying need

The structures must allow participants to identify where the needs of the workforce and of the organization lie, and concentrate on these. Some workforce and much political participation is peripheral, in that it addresses marginal issues, or the marginal elements of significant issues. This may be because the agenda is set by those who are not genuinely committed to, or do not understand, the intentions of participation.

Accessibility

The structures must be accessible, both physically and psychologically, to all the workforce in appropriate ways. This can imply adaptation of language, methods of communication systems, workplace traditions, and so on. The implication of Lukes' (1974) work is that the powerless will collude in any attempts to exclude them – in simple terms, by learning to 'know their place'. This has to be resisted, sometimes over long periods of time.

Information

Information is critical to participation – it has to be needs-led, appropriate and, again, accessible.

Efficiency

Amidst all the sophisticated advice given in books such as this, it is sometimes overlooked that the primary function of management is to manage. The efficiency of the organization is a key focus for the leadership role, and one that can be monitored and evaluated.

In attempting to evaluate the relative efficiency of European railway networks, Pestieau (1993) identified three factors that need to be taken into account: managerial effectiveness, the relative autonomy of individual networks to organize themselves to maximize operational efficiency, and technical progress. Managerial effectiveness, of course, can be measured by customer/client and staff satisfaction, and also by the amount of time, effort and other resources (including financial ones) put in versus satisfaction with the outcomes. Both user and staff satisfaction can be measured most finely when people are accustomed to being part of such an evaluation process. Voluntary organizations have increasing autonomy as they move from a grant-aided to a contract culture. Voluntary organizations encompass a wide range of preparedness for the range of information technology available to them; smaller organizations largely lacking the capital backing to take full advantage of the market.

It is important that organizations do measure their own efficiency in these or other ways.

Financial management

In my experience, in no area of work do voluntary organizations vary more widely than in their approach to financial management. Some produce polished documents based on computerized accounts with sophisticated forecasting, while others appear to be unable to produce a working budget. Performance in this field bears no relationship to size. Some of the best-prepared organizations are among the smallest, while some branches of national organizations have no financial records whatsoever. As has been suggested, the prerequisite of effective financial management is financial understanding, and a number of organizations fail to address this basic requirement. In fact, the finances of most voluntary organizations, especially those delivering a single service, are a comparatively simple matter. Many have one source of income only, the grant (latterly the contract). Many have a straightforward pattern of expenditure, as shown on the sample budget sheet in Fig. 5.2.

In a dual- or multi-purpose organization, the columns will represent expenditure on the different projects managed, making it easy to identify actual

EXPENDITURE	A	B	C	D
STAFFING				
Salaries (gross, inc. on-costs) Manager	15,000	6,500		
Asst. Manager		19,000		
Admin.		11,600		
Training & Consultancy		10,000		
Sessional/volunteer expenses	3,000	9,600		
Employers' insurance				
PREMISES				
Rent (projected @ 250 sq. ft @ £5.50)	(1375)			
Charges	1,000	600		
OFFICE EXPENSES				
Telephone & postage	720	1,400		
Printing & stationery	262	1,100		
Publicity		3,000		
Office equipment – rental				
– maintenance		500		
Insurance	100	900		
Professional fees	800	5,500		
OPERATIONAL EXPENSES				
Sundries		2,300		
Management/Admin. fees				
Contingency		3,000		
Total Expenditure	21,882	75,000		
INCOME				
Grant	23,000			
Contract		75,000		
Earnings				
Management/Admin. fees				
Total Income	23,000	75,000		

Figure 5.2 Sample budget sheet (pounds sterling)

costs. Very few smaller voluntary organizations will need a more complex structure than that shown in Fig. 5.2. However, it is sometimes necessary, where an organization takes on a contract and funding to deliver a discrete service, for a calculation of proportionate charging of parts of the central or administration costs. This may be done by a rough estimate of time, space or actual costs incurred (see, for example, Callaghan 1992). It is important that the calculations on which these estimates are based (however much they are guessed) are kept, so that they can be shared with funders and used as a baseline in the future.

It is an absolute requirement that an effective and ethical organization has adequate control over its finances, that it monitors income and expenditure, that it devolves spending to appropriate levels within the organization, and that it forecasts future income and expenditure, and plans accordingly. Too often members of small organizations have said, 'We have so little money, and it's all eaten up the same way each year, that planning would be a waste of time'. To which the response should be, 'The less you have, the more you need to plan'. Effective control assumes, at least, an annual exercise in forecasting and planning conducted by the whole management committee/board.

So it is important that the entire management committee takes part in the formulation of a business plan. Once a basic structure such as the one described in Chapter 2 is in place, the format can be made more practical and, to some extent, simplified. The organization needs to recognize that a business plan has a number of audiences. First, it is the document which acts as a route plan for the management team, and a handbook for the staff, to remind everyone what the aims and priorities of the organization are during the current year. Second, it is a document which explains the organization in its current state to existing and potential funders, shows them the actual and potential income and expenditure, and guarantees them that the organization is run in such an efficient and effective manner that the purposeful expenditure of their money, for the agreed purpose, is assured. Third, it is a brief summary of the organization for potential clients, staff and networking organizations. The contents suggested are adapted from Williams (1993):

1 *Introduction*: a very brief history of the origins, development and aims of the organization.
2 *Structure*: a description of the management (voluntary) and staffing, and key issues for management.
3 *The service*: a description of the service provided and the target client group.
4 *Marketing*: current funding and opportunities for development, strategies for self-presentation of the organization, networking, relationships with potential funders.
5 *Operational details*: the organization base(s), costing and charging arrangements (costing of one of the services delivered will be based upon the budgeting exercise described above), recruitment of staff.
6 *Financial analysis*: current financial issues and projections for the future.
7 *Objectives*: the priorities agreed by the management committee for the coming year(s), including any planned growth, strategies to ensure stability and financial viability, developments in the quality of the service, and strategies to ensure the integrity of the organization and value for money in its service delivery.
8 *Budget sheet*: details of the planned expenditure and income for the current year, as above.

The contract

As contracts continue to replace grants as the funding mechanism for voluntary organizations, especially for those engaged in direct service delivery, the question of the format of the contract itself becomes a major issue. As the voluntary sector becomes more experienced in these matters, we can hope that they have more control over the process. The NCVO's 'Advancing Good Management' project made clear that the majority of local authorities were dictating not only the nature and pace of change, but also the nature and composition of the contracts. This need not, however, be the case. In Sandwell, for example, the SSD, together with its legal advisers, was happy to allow draft contracts to be drawn up by the organizations themselves. These were then discussed with social services officers and amended so as to meet with council legal requirements. In the event, the resulting format was in two parts: a statement of the agreement in lay language, accessible to voluntary sector staff and volunteers and council officers, while the legal details were confined to a separate section. For the structure, the list of inclusions in Adirondack (1990) was followed:

1 Introduction, including parties to the contract, dates, etc.
2 Services to be provided, an agreed statement (the agreed basis for funding under the earlier grant regime), the clients and quality standards.
3 A statement of equality of opportunity, including plans to broaden the cultural and geographical base.
4 Procedures for consultation between the two parties.
5 Arrangements for monitoring and evaluating the contracted service.
6 The premises to be used for service delivery.
7 The equipment required.
8 Costs, charges and payment arrangements.
9 Financial monitoring and review.
10 Staffing provisions and support, including training and appraisal arrangements.
11 Insurance.
12 Enforcement and arrangements to settle disputes.
13 Arrangements for review, variation and extension.
14 Signatures and dates.

In some local authorities, there has been a confusing assortment of arrangements with social services over staff and premises. A number of organizations have been provided with staff seconded from the council. This has often occurred in an attempt to save the jobs of contracted local authority staff whose positions have been threatened in the annual cuts in local government funding over recent years. While some voluntary organizations have been happy to employ staff on behalf of the council, increasingly anomalies have arisen. Despite the voluntary sector's gradual move towards parity in employment with the authorities, sometimes these anomalies have been financial – council staff being paid on different (usually more generous) scales, with different (usually more favourable) terms and conditions, including holidays. Occasionally, however, this has resulted in managerial problems, whereby staff, in the event of a dispute with their placement manager, have argued that they aren't really employed by the organization and have appealed to their home department. In a contract, existing arrangements can be recognized, their financial worth calculated and the strategy for reorganization laid down. Similarly, many voluntary organizations have operated from premises owned or rented by the local authority, and with resources and equipment owned and lent by the authority.

Such anomalies need to be ironed out to ensure that the voluntary sector receives no hidden subsidy when competing with private organizations in tendering for council or health authority contracts. While the voluntary sector might retain some advantages as competitive bidders, as far as the law allows, it is important that the subsidies and advantages should be visible to all.

Therefore, a contract must have the following fundamental characteristics if it is to act effectively as a practical and legal agreement between purchaser and provider:

1 It must be couched in readily accessible language.
2 It must be comprehensive.
3 It must be clear in its expectations, but flexible in application.

The voluntary organization with a future

The regeneration and prosperity of the voluntary sector in the next few years will depend upon its ability to demonstrate the qualities discussed in this chapter:

- A clear set of values, represented by explicit statements and internal operations.
- An increasing commitment to democratic and accountable management.
- A lessening reliance on bureaucratic methods of management.
- Staying in touch with the ethical roots of the organization.
- Identifying, valuing and exploiting individual skills and qualities.
- Absorbing change into the organization.
- Observing the quality 'markers' of successful organizations.
- Defining and targeting organizational efficiency.
- Ensuring a clear legal/contractual basis for external relationships.

A COMMITMENT TO QUALITY

- What is quality?
- Quality standards
- Evaluation
- Components of quality
- Code of conduct
- Appraisal
- Investors in people
- Equal opportunities

Quality is much talked about and much written about. In our everyday experience over the last decade or so, we have seen something of a revolution in attitudes to service in this country. Hotels and restaurants, shops and garages, banks and the post office, have turned the focus on customer need, largely because they have had to. Competition in a period of alternating inflation and recession concentrates the mind. In the public sector, a greater commitment to accountability has brought about a whole range of initiatives designed to allow the public to assess and evaluate the services they receive.

This book does not intend to review the history of quality assurance; this has been done elsewhere (see, for example, Crosby 1979; Deming 1986; Peters 1987). This chapter introduces a number of ways in which concepts of quality can be used to sharpen up the organization and delivery of services within the voluntary sector.

Quality standards

The areas in which quality standards might be applied to voluntary sector organizations delivering services were introduced in Chapter 2. One voluntary organization uses the following set of quality standards, against which both the service and the organization could be measured.

Organizational

1 *Training* of staff, volunteers and management committee
 (i) Care workers will meet together on a monthly basis. The agenda

will be open to input from the management committee, organizer, coordinator and care workers. The organizer will ensure that care workers are able to attend at least every 2 months.

(ii) Care workers will be required to undertake training to:
  (a) familiarize themselves with the aims and objectives of the project;
  (b) consider issues of equal opportunities;
  (c) consider the implications of the project and their work for the users and for their relationships with their clients;
  (d) consider their own personal and professional development within the project.

(iii) Workshops for staff and the management committee addressing issues raised by the work of the project will take place every 6 months. These will be formulated around issues identified by staff, the management committee and the evaluation reports.

(iv) Staff will adhere to a code of conduct setting rules and guidelines on relationships with users, including conduct, dress, language, etc.

(v) Staff will be offered opportunities to participate in other ways in the management of the project.

2 *User participation* in management
  (i) Wherever possible, users and/or carers will be included in the policy-making and decision-making processes.

3 *Terms and conditions* of employment
  (i) All staff will have terms and conditions of employment which are comparable with those of employees of the social services department with equivalent duties and responsibilities.
  (ii) Staff have the right to understand the terms and conditions of employment.
  (iii) Terms and conditions of employment, once agreed, will not be altered without negotiation.
  (iv) Management staff will ensure, wherever possible, that employees work the agreed hours.

4 *Job descriptions*
  (i) All staff will have job descriptions which are reviewed annually.
  (ii) Job descriptions will, wherever possible, be comparable to those of equivalent staff of the social services department.

5 *Equal opportunities employment*
  (i) The project will adhere to a policy of equal opportunities employment.

6 *Financial controls*
  (i) The management committee will agree an annual budget for the project.
  (ii) Project staff will exercise financial control over project

expenditure within budget heads agreed by the management committee.

(iii) Management committee will receive financial reports on at least a 3 monthly basis.

7 *Staff supervision,* inc. appraisal

(i) An appraisal procedure will be followed for all staff of the project. The procedure will be subject to review at 6 monthly intervals.

(ii) All care workers will have access to management staff to discuss issues arising out of their employment. During normal working weeks, appointments will be offered within 48 hours of the request.

(iii) Management staff will encourage care workers to make use of the formal and informal support offered by them.

(iv) Staff *support* will be non-judgemental.

(v) Administrative procedures will be evaluated regularly to ensure that they support the work of the project. Evaluation will include care workers and, where appropriate, users and/or carers.

(vi) Principles of good management will be applied consistently between and with all staff.

Service

8 *Client assessment*

(i) All individuals referred to the service will receive an assessment visit from the project organizer within 3 days of receipt of the referral. Assessment will follow the procedure laid down.

(ii) The assessment may result in a care package which will be negotiated and agreed between the user, his or her carer(s) and the project organizer.

(iii) Care workers will monitor the service provided in terms of appropriateness and outcome throughout the period of support.

(iv) Users will be assessed by the project organizer at intervals of 3 months.

(v) The assessment procedure will be reviewed at intervals of 12 months.

(vi) The management committee will have a policy of prioritization which will enable staff to determine the eligibility of users for the service.

(vii) Where possible, care workers will be allocated to users in accordance with the needs of the user.

(viii) Good practice in care management will be applied consistently between and with all users.

9 *Written procedures*

(i) An assessment procedure will be followed with all referrals and users. The assessment procedure will be reviewed at intervals of 12 months. It will be evaluated against other available procedures, including the local authority SSD assessment, and those recommended by the Social Services Inspectorate.

(ii) A complaints procedure will be in place. All users and their carers will be informed of the procedure on negotiation of the care package, and reminded of its existence as appropriate by their care workers.

(iii) The project will also have in place a code of conduct for staff, and a procedure for health and safety of users and staff.

10 *Equal opportunities*

(i) An equal opportunities policy and procedures will be followed with users.

(ii) All methods of communication within and about the project, whether verbal or written, will be couched in language appropriate to the intended audience.

11 *Services additional* to the core function

(i) Where possible and appropriate, the service will perform over and above the minimum requirements of the work specified in both quantity and quality.

12 *Building conditions and facilities*

(i) The offices, social and conference areas used by the project will be maintained so as to be a welcoming and professional environment for staff and visitors.

(ii) All premises used by the project will be assessed regularly for 'fitness for purpose'.

13 *Reporting, monitoring, evaluation and statistics*

(i) The services provided by the project will be evaluated against the objectives at 6 monthly intervals by an independent consultant. The resultant report will be available to all workers.

(ii) Statistics of the client group will be maintained by management staff, and will be regularly reported to the management committee.

(iii) Statistics relating to the care workers will be maintained by management staff and will be regularly reported to the management committee.

(iv) Information about users will be maintained by management staff so as to be *accurate, confidential* but *accessible* to the relevant staff and care workers at need. Accuracy will be maintained by regular checking of information held against users', carers' and care workers' perceptions.

14 *Networking*

(i) Management staff will meet regularly with: management committee, other statutory and voluntary agencies providing or coordinating community care in the locality, and other organizations involved in similar work elsewhere in the country.

(ii) Staff and committee members will participate in local and national networks for sharing information and developing services within the field of community care, and in the work of any local federation or development agency.

These quality standards can, in many instances, be quite closely measured. Others are deliberately less precise. This may be intentional, as some standards may be more impressionistic, about ethos or relationships, rather than statistics. In this example, the development of standards was at an early stage. In some areas, the organization had not yet developed procedures to which it was committed. In others, procedures were in place but in the early stages of development and experimentation. With a set of more or less measurable standards, evaluation can be conducted against a set of clear and agreed criteria. This will enable any evaluator to:

1 Make judgements about the extent to which quality standards are regularly met.
2 Make recommendations about action to be taken.
3 Comment on the appropriateness and comprehensiveness of the standards, and make recommendations for amendments and additions.

The evaluator, then, has three main functions:

1 To confirm that the management committee and staff regularly monitor their procedures (i.e. to ensure that what they say happens, happens).
2 To make judgements about the extent to which the standards to which the organization is committed are achieved.
3 To assess the relevance and appropriateness of the standards, and recommend changes or emendations to them.

How, then, does an organization set about identifying the standards to which it believes it should commit itself? There are two useful starting points. The first is a consideration, and simplification, of the statutory or contractual responsibilities of the organization. Does the committee effectively monitor the organization and the service it delivers? This can be subdivided into the areas of operation listed in Table 2.1 (p. 13). The approach is to ask, 'What should the management committee know in relation to this area of its responsibilities?'

1 *Operation of the management committee*: organization development plan, committee and sub committee terms of reference, committee/staff responsibilities.
2 *Funding*: funding sources and terms of agreements, potential funders, relationships with funders.
3 *Service*: service delivery and development, strategic plans, action plans.
4 *Staffing*: staff roll, gender, ethnic origin, responsibilities.
5 *Employment*: terms and conditions of employment, job descriptions, procedures, appraisals.
6 *Financial controls*: knowledge and information about income and expenditure, evaluation of historical expenditure, offering of real budget choices/options, regular statements.
7 *Development*: strategic plans.

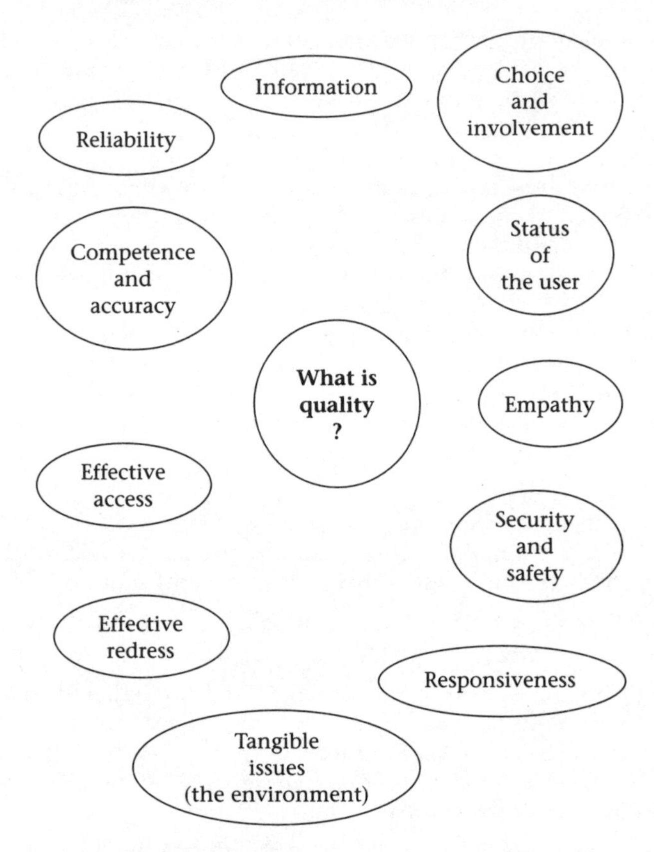

Figure 6.1 Some components of quality
Reproduced from Lawrie (1995) with the permission of the Directory of Social Change.

The element of quality of service is omitted here, as it forms the basis of the second starting point for quality assurance (see Fig. 6.1).

The management committee and staff could also begin by looking at each of the 'components' of quality in the model, and deciding what standards they would set in each area. It should be emphasized that such an approach does not necessarily imply drastic change within the operation of an organization. Many of the procedures incorporated into this model will be up and running as standard practice. What this does is two-fold. It organizes the procedures into a coherent structure, and it provides a model whereby a lay manager without the professional background of the staff can evaluate the organization's effectiveness. This model is therefore applicable to any business or service provider in any sector. In each component, the committee will find a series of questions to be asked, and procedures to adopt. (The quoted statements following each component are taken from Lawrie 1995.)

1 *Information*: 'The availability of information (in different forms) which explains the organization and the services in a simple way'.
   - Are all users familiar with the history, structure and purposes of the organization?
   - Is information given out according to what people want and need (rather than what the organization thinks people should want and need)?
   - Is there regular contact with users, both written and verbal?
   - Is there a mechanism for publicizing the work of the organization?
   - Are all staff aware of all the relevant structures and procedures, codes of conduct, development plans?
   - Is all information presented in the appropriate language(s)?
   - Is information presented in a variety of ways?
   - Is information 'tested out' on users to see if it communicates effectively?
2 *Reliability*: 'The knowledge that a service will be carried out as agreed and to an agreed time'.
   - Is there a set of procedures which guarantee consistency of service, for example assessment, code of conduct, health and safety?
   - Is there a contract between the organization and individual users?
   - Is there internal and external monitoring and evaluation of the service?
   - Does the organization seek to improve its service by networking with other agencies?
   - Is a complaints procedure used?
   - Is individual usage reviewed regularly?
   - Are there guidelines for response times to communications?
3 *Competence and accuracy*: 'The staff have the required skill and knowledge to provide a service competently'.
   - All communications will be checked for accuracy of content and presentation.
   - Managers will check samples of work conducted by service workers.
   - Staff will check regularly with all users of information as to the relevance and accuracy of information.
   - All staff will receive a period of induction into the aims and procedures of the organization.
   - All staff will receive copies of all relevant procedures.
   - All staff will receive opportunities for training and development, both 'refresher' courses and in new skills.
   - Staff will be allocated to a training/support group and to an experienced mentor.
4 *Effective access*: 'The first point of contact with the organization encourages the person to use the service, and the service feels "approachable". Also there is an equality of access amongst users'.
   - The organization has an equal opportunities policy and procedures.
   - The organization has a complaints procedure.
   - The organization has a handbook for users describing the service, its monitoring and evaluation.
   - Statistics on the age, gender, ethnic origin and residence of users are regularly reviewed.

- All staff make positive efforts to welcome, and to listen to, users.
- There is no labelling of 'troublesome users'.
- Appointments are available with all appropriate staff at short notice.
- Reception areas and interview areas are welcoming.
- Space is available for confidential interviews.
- Relevant telephone numbers and addresses are readily available.
- Appropriate language and languages are used.
- Telephone and correspondence answering is welcoming and positive.
- The presentation of a positive view of the organization does not preclude or deny the raising of complaints and queries.

5 *Effective redress*: 'When things go wrong or when a user feels that they have had poor service or unfair treatment they are able to quickly have things put right'.
   - The organization has a complaints procedure.
   - The organization has a handbook for users describing access to the service, its monitoring and evaluation.
   - Users are encouraged to raise issues with staff at all levels of the service.
   - Staff understand that complaints are material for improving service quality.
   - There is a written contract between the organization and its users, with a statement of users' rights.

6 *Tangible issues*: 'The physical appearance of the service'.
   - Offices and other premises used by the service are, and appear, 'fit for purpose'.
   - Equipment is appropriate and 'fit for purpose'.
   - All staff (particularly first contact staff) are aware of the importance of presentational issues.
   - All written communications are presented in an appropriately professional manner.
   - Premises and equipment are regularly evaluated by an external adviser.
   - All staff evaluate their working conditions regularly.
   - The premises budget gives due weight to the status of the user.
   - There is a premises and equipment development plan.

7 *Responsiveness*: 'The willingness and ability of staff to provide a service in a personal and thoughtful way'.
   - There is a code of conduct agreed and kept by staff, and communicated to users.
   - Every user has a 'key worker'.
   - Response times to communications are communicated to users and strictly adhered to by staff.
   - Staff have regular opportunities to share issues about relationships with users.

8 *Security and safety*: 'A freedom from danger, risk or accident. Personal security. Confidentiality'.
   - A health and safety procedure is published, followed and reviewed regularly.
   - Premises and equipment are 'fit for purpose'.
   - Users understand that their safety and security are priorities with staff.

- There are regular safety exercises (e.g. fire drills).
- Users are exposed to an appropriate, acceptable and agreed level of risk in activities.
- Users are exposed to an appropriate, acceptable and agreed level of challenge in their own development.
- The different appropriate levels of confidentiality in dealings between staff and users are agreed and understood.
- Written and computerized material is accessible only to appropriate staff.
- Users have a right to see any stored information about themselves.

9 *Empathy*: 'The degree to which staff listen to and explain things to individual users'.
   - Key workers are encouraged to act as advocates for the users for whom they are responsible.
   - Staff training focuses on users' circumstances and needs.
   - Users feel that the organization 'sits alongside' them and gives them appropriate support in their contacts with other agencies.
   - Evaluation of the service includes user perceptions.

10 *Choice and involvement*: 'The ability of a user to influence the type and level of service provided'.
   - Users are involved in management committee decisions.
   - A users' consultative group meets regularly, independently of staff.
   - There are opportunities for users to make choices at appropriate levels of the service.
   - All users are informed of, and have explained to them, all the options open to them.
   - The aims of the service are regularly reviewed with users.

11 *Status of the user*: 'The degree of respect given to the client. What does it feel like to be a user?'
   - The reciprocal nature of dependency between user and service is recognized by staff and users.
   - Users are given priority (over, for example, other agencies) in access to staff.
   - There is an agreed and evaluated written contract between the organization and its users, with a statement of users' rights and entitlements.
   - Staff training will focus on users' needs and rights.

The adoption of a model such as this (suitably adapted to the users' needs which an organization is meeting) will guarantee, as far as possible, that service focuses on a continual improvement in quality.

Once quality standards are in place, they can, more or less accurately, be measured by an external evaluator. The overarching question for the evaluator is: 'To what extent are the stated aims of the organization being achieved?' Evaluators will produce a review of the service, followed by a series of action points to be addressed. An example of a set of action points presented to an organization at the end of an evaluation against agreed quality standards is given in Table 6.1. As this evaluation was of an organization experiencing a period of rapid change, many of the action points are concerned with review

Table 6.1 Action points

1	Review attendance at staff monthly meetings; take action to ensure that all workers can attend at least every other meeting
2	Review training programme to ensure updates and team-building work for all, especially new entrants. Consider training in basic first aid and in 'meeting new users'
3	Present code of conduct to workers. Provide workshop day to include discussion and agreement
4	Plan and evaluate carers' consultative committee meetings
5	Discuss with staff the need for a representative structure
6	Record staff's 'ideal' working patterns, discuss viability and set targets
7	Review job descriptions
8	Review financial arrangements: budget forecasting, controls
9	Calculate unit costs and compare with comparable services elsewhere
10	Review appraisal procedure
11	Put in place emergency contact procedures for evenings and weekends
12	Agree time limits for client assessment (initial and review)
13	Finalize eligibility criteria
14	Review and finalize assessment procedure
15	Prepare complaints procedure

or setting up procedures. An organization in a settled period would expect to have clearer single actions to follow.

Code of conduct

In all of the above, it is assumed that staff have a code of conduct against which to evaluate their own work. In an organization committed to quality, the code will focus on the needs and rights of users, while protecting the rights of staff. The code provides consistency and reliability of the service, so that users know what to expect both from and between workers. The code also protects the quality of the service, provides security to staff in their assessment of their own performance, and protects them from exploitation. Such a code can be prepared with staff at a training workshop with an experienced trainer, with inputs from staff at all levels of the organization, and with wide-ranging experience. Its development, therefore, can be good training practice – recognizing the needs of all staff within the organization, benefiting from and valuing their varied experience and skills, while acknowledging that the status of the user is paramount. In the following example, due to the nature of the organization and the early stage of its development, the needs of users were represented by staff and trainers, although best practice would ensure that users or their representatives participated formally in the process. In the example below, care workers were asked to consider the difficult decisions they had to make in their work, and the actual and potential conflicts they were meeting. The code was therefore compiled out of actual experience.

In any code of conduct, there needs to be absolute clarity about what are rules – the breach of which could, ultimately, lead to disciplinary procedures – and what is advice. Both rules and guidelines need to be explained, in terms of what they mean and why we have them. It is important that a code is as far as possible a list of 'DOs', not a catalogue of 'DON'Ts'. The feeling that the rules of an organization belong to the workers will not be generated if staff are faced with an intimidating series of proscriptions. Where a clear DON'T is necessary, an equally clear explanation for the rule is essential. This code is, of course, prepared for domiciliary care workers, but can be adapted for most caring situations.

Code of conduct

Rules and guidelines for care workers in a home visiting service

The purpose of rules and guidelines is to ensure that the service provided by care workers is as sensitive, appropriate and of as high quality as possible, and for you to be clear about your role and its boundaries.

1 Timing

(a) *Rules* – Be punctual. A delay or early arrival of even a few minutes can be upsetting for the client. If you are unavoidably delayed, always explain and reassure.

(b) *Guidelines* – Arriving more than 5 minutes early is *too* early, and arriving more than 5 minutes late is *too* late. Do not overstay your welcome or be coerced into staying longer. The longer you stay, the more you will lose the focus of your call.

Try to make time to say goodbye specifically and leave promptly. If you are unable to make a call, the project organizer or the project coordinator should be notified at least 24 hours before the call. In the extreme case of an emergency, telephone the office as soon as you can.

2 Behaviour

(a) *Rules*
  (i) Dress must be clean, practical and suitable. Denim jeans, mini skirts and low necklines are not permissible.
  (ii) Hair should be tidy and practical for the tasks in hand.
  (iii) Footwear should be suitable and practical for the tasks in hand. Neither shoes with stiletto heels nor mules are permissible *or* safe.
  (iv) Excessive amounts of jewellery must not be worn. Chains, rings and bracelets can be dangerous.
  (v) Nail polish is not permissible.
  (vi) Do not form intimate or sexual relationships with clients.

(vii) Maintain confidentiality. Anything a client tells you should be shared only with appropriate members of the organization.

(b) *Guidelines* – check with clients:

- what name they would like you to call them;
- what name you are both comfortable with them calling you.

Do not 'dump' your own problems on clients. It is not helpful for someone who is ill or depressed to hear a great deal about your problems. Share, but don't overload.

Take great care that any touching that takes place is comfortable for both you and the client. Never let touching become ambiguous. If there is a personal attraction between yourself and your client, or between a client and you, discuss this immediately with the project organizer or project coordinator.

3 Tasks

(a) *Rules* – Only perform tasks which have been negotiated at the assessment and which you are briefed to carry out.

(b) *Guidelines* – Do the tasks with a good feeling and as much commitment as you can. If you are being asked to do more tasks than you can manage, talk to the project organizer or project coordinator.

4 Valuables

(a) *Rules*

(i) Only go into private space (e.g. wallets or money drawers) with direct instruction from the client.

(ii) Do not lend money to, or borrow money from, clients under any circumstances.

(iii) Never hold keys, unless directed to do so by the project organizer or project coordinator.

(iv) Do not give presents to the client. Do not accept large presents from the client. It may sometimes be sensitive to accept small gifts such as sweets and talcum powder, but all gifts *must* be reported to the project organizer. This is for *your* protection.

(b) *Guidelines* – Exchanging birthday and seasonal cards is acceptable. If you do shopping for a client in advance of receiving money, keep the receipt for payment. If you are not repaid, do not shop again without money in advance, and notify the project organizer. Use the agreed procedure for handling clients' money.

5 Medication

(a) *Rules* – Never administer prescribed drugs unless directed to do so via a Medipac facility by the project organizer or project coordinator.

(b) *Guidelines* – Inaccurate administration of medication can kill. If you are asked by clients for drugs, you must *always* contact the project organizer immediately.

6 Finally . . .

If you are worried or puzzled about anything to do with being a care worker, talk to the project organizer or project coordinator – that is what they are there for.

We affirm that everyone is entitled to privacy, dignity, independence, choice, rights and fulfilment.

Your work with a client makes a genuine difference to his or her quality of life. Be proud of it.

Appraisal

Alongside the code of conduct, an appraisal system helps to ensure the delivery of a quality service by giving staff a framework of knowledge and practical support. Like codes of conduct, appraisal systems need to be developed as far as possible with and by staff in order to achieve an acceptable format. The role-playing of appraisal sessions can help both to identify potential problems and to practise appraisal interviews.

There are a number of problems associated with the introduction and implementation of appraisal systems which are committed to being support systems for staff, and which aim to improve the quality of service delivery. First, appraisal can be seen to be part of a supervisory and disciplinary system, designed to identify weaknesses, with the ultimate sanction of the application of disciplinary procedures, with the issues raised in appraisal as part of the 'evidence'. In one of the discussions setting up an appraisal system in a voluntary organization, one member of the board described how an appraisal interview had been used to produce a damaging report. He had explained to his manager how a number of short-term family problems had led to an occasional lack of concentration, and so to a feeling that he was not always performing at his best. While this information was received sympathetically, a subsequent report announced that this officer was not working to his potential because of personal problems. No other evidence was used in this judgement and the officer, justifiably, felt cheated and betrayed by a system which he will never use honestly again. Appraisal must deal exclusively with improving performance by offering appropriate support systems; most commonly these will be training opportunities, but they may take the form of internal support systems, or changes in job responsibility or line management. The material raised in appraisal must always remain confidential within the system and must never be used outside it for other purposes without the agreement of both appraiser and appraised, except in the very unusual circumstance of something illegal being revealed. This agreement must be reached between the parties involved before the process begins.

Second, appraisal can be used as part of a work record. Appraisal is not, however, meant to achieve an objective judgement of an employee's performance. Indeed, the great advantage of appraisal is that it is largely subjective and concerned with people's feelings about, and confidence in, their work. Few employees will try to judge their work performance honestly and share that judgement with anyone else, let alone a manager, if they know that such judgements can be used against them. Appraisal, therefore, is not meant to be part of a work assessment process for any purpose, least of all to contribute towards decisions on salary increases. At the end of his appraisal, the officer cited above received a report which summed up his performance as 'only satisfactory'. What this phrase – reminiscent of school reports 30 years ago – actually means might puzzle the finest brains. If a performance is satisfactory, it is satisfactory, full stop. The production of mark-sheets and misleadingly simplistic assessments of performance have no place in a supportive appraisal system.

The third problem that appraisal systems face is that they are largely introduced, and operated, by those at the top of the workplace hierarchy. Although this may be for the best of motives, there will often be suspicion among the workforce, if not downright hostility. Communications need to be absolutely clear about the purposes, there needs to be negotiation about the need for appraisal, as well as about its format, and the workforce needs to be involved in the development of the scheme. Suspicions can sometimes be allayed by the inclusion of upwards appraisal (not to be confused with upwards assessment, which may also have its place, but is nothing to do with supportive appraisal). However, the only means of ensuring that appraisal is used as intended will be by developing trust and confidence in the process over time.

The fourth obstacle to effective appraisal is a more personal one, that of developing in employees the ability to be aware of their performance and to evaluate it honestly. This demands that there is a system of breaking down the tasks, and the expectations, placed on staff, and training them to evaluate their performance as objectively – and with as little defensiveness – as possible. Such self-awareness is an art in itself and needs patient and sensitive development.

For some, even more difficult than self-evaluation is evaluation of others or of an organization's systems and procedures. This may particularly be the case in the voluntary sector, where so much appears to run on goodwill. Certainly, training exercises and games which require an element of competition can founder when people are so nice to each other and so pleased (and often grateful) to have a job, or to have the chance to be involved in voluntary work. Trainers will remember the game Starpower, devised by Gary Shirts, popular in the 1970s. This game relied on simulated, and rigged, trading sessions, with plastic chips representing money, to replicate the social inequity in the distribution of goods. Judiciously managed, the game could – and frequently did – degenerate into near violent confrontation, particularly so when the outcomes of the game were extended into real life, by rewarding 'winners' with a full three-course meal, and punishing 'losers' with a slice of bread and a glass of water. The only time in the author's experience that Starpower 'failed' was when it was played with a group from a Christian centre. When they realized the structure of the game, all the 'wealthy' players distributed their plastic chips equally among the group. However, through such training exercises, staff do develop the skills of analysing and criticizing in order to do their own jobs well; for example, evaluating the suitability of a home environment for a disabled person, or the fitness of a relative to provide care.

If these difficulties are addressed in the formulation and implementation of a scheme, appraisal has the capacity to give people an element of control over their working lives that can transform their attitude, not only to the workplace, but to the users. It is important that an evaluation of the procedure is built in, preferably on, say, a 6 monthly basis while it is 'bedding in'. The following responses were reported from an evaluation meeting conducted with six care workers after their first (and in some cases second) appraisal experience:

It's a genuine chance to develop.

It's a chance of a one-to-one talk with management.

You feel what you're doing is really important.

It creates a growing record of my good work.

It shows management have good information about care workers.

It shows management are monitoring what is going on, what you do *is* noticed.

I found out what appraisal *was*.

You could have a fresh discussion each time; it wasn't just the same things repeated from last time.

It was nice to have an outsider (a member of the management committee) hear it all.

It's the first time I've ever been complimented.

Some of the aspects of the procedure were less popular:

I couldn't understand the form.

The form frightened me.

The form made me laugh.

I didn't like the big table (used for interviews) – it felt unfriendly.

I felt worked up before I arrived.

I felt anxious at first.

I didn't know the first time what it was.

As can be seen, the problems were largely structural ones which can be dealt with. An appraisal procedure may mean employing what has, perhaps, largely been seen as a professional process with people who have traditionally seen themselves – and perhaps been encouraged to see themselves – as unskilled, low-value workers with jobs, not careers. There will be obstacles in the very processes (the use of paper responses, official forms, interviews, etc.) and these need to be addressed by the organization in the setting-up stages. Much of the material used in this organization was based upon that developed by Investors in People in their 'appraisal' of organizations. Because Investors in People addresses itself to all the workers in the organization, it has developed more appropriate ways of addressing staff with different levels of experience of evaluation.

The organization handbook

Every voluntary organization needs straightforward ways of communicating, on several different levels, with users, their carers and potential users, staff, funders, other agencies in similar work, the media and the general public. In addition to the development plan and records of organizational procedures, there should be a general introductory handbook. This will be a snapshot view of the organization and its work at a particular time, and need not be a particularly glossy publication. It should be updatable cheaply every year, and may be linked to a report prepared for the annual general meeting. It might include all the organizational quality standards and the means by which they are achieved, and may be structured as follows:

- The mission statement, or statement of aims, and objectives.
- A statement of equal opportunities.
- An outline of the service(s) provided.
- Arrangements for monitoring and evaluation of the service.
- Training of staff.
- Examples of the work done by the organization.
- Criteria for access to the service.

Investors in People

Investors in People (IIP) is a national quality standard for employers, administered by Investors in People UK, which is administered and assessed through the local Training and Enterprise Councils (TECs) (Local Enterprise Companies in Scotland). IIP was launched in 1991, and focuses on the induction, training and development of staff throughout the organization. There are four principles to the standard, each of which is accompanied by a number of performance indicators:

1 *Commitment*: the employer makes a public commitment from the top to help all employees to achieve its business objectives. This involves a written organization plan setting out goals and targets for all employees, and communicating the vision of where the organization is going.
2 *Planning*: the employer regularly reviews the training and development needs of all employees. Training resources must be clearly identified, and each employee agrees training and development needs with the management.
3 *Action*: the employer takes action to train and develop individuals on recruitment and throughout their employment. Action focuses on the

training needs of new recruits and the continual development of existing staff, encouraging them to contribute to identifying and meeting their own development needs.
4 *Evaluation*: an IIP employer evaluates the investment in training and development to assess achievement and improve future effectiveness. Investment in training and its outcomes are regularly reviewed against goals and targets, leading to renewed commitment and target setting.

In order to be recognized as an IIP employer, the organization makes a commitment to its local TEC, producing an action plan to show where it falls short of the standard and how it intends to achieve it. TECs provide a 'toolkit' to assist in this process, including a set of questionnaires which can be used with staff to identify what their perception of the organization is, and its systems for supporting staff. The action plan is usually put together with the help of an adviser, preferably one who has attended one of the recognized courses in IIP consultancy. When the TEC has received the commitment and approved the action plan, the organization sets out to 'fill in the gaps'. Again, the support of a recognized adviser can be helpful throughout this process, which may take anything from 6 months to several years. When lead staff think it is ready, the organization will return to the TEC with a portfolio of written evidence demonstrating how each indicator is now met. Assessment is conducted by a recognized consultant appointed by the TEC and is based initially on the portfolio, but more importantly on interviews conducted with a sample of all the staff of the organization. The assessor then makes a recommendation to a panel appointed by the TEC, which either does or does not award the organization IIP employer status. Organizations must show that they meet *all* the indicators to achieve recognition; there is no such thing as 'partial' recognition.

If the organization is committed to achieving the standard, the action plan will easily accord with the existing development plan, and the portfolio will be a collection of documents which form part of the organization's built-in procedures.

Victoria Visiting Venture made its initial organizational audit and commitment to IIP in October 1994, and was assessed in April 1995, gaining recognition the following month. This was an unusually short time to draw up and achieve an action plan, but many of the indicators were being met as part of a consultancy project which had been under way for more than 2 years. The major task the organization had to achieve was to draw up an all-embracing business/development plan which brought together all the elements of the organization and set targets for them. The portfolio comprised all the existing documents: the business plan, a record of policies and procedures, the IIP indicators with evidence to demonstrate how they were being met, the results of the managers' and employees' surveys, project objectives and quality standards, the organization handbook and two evaluation reports. The policies and procedures included the complaints procedure, equal opportunities policy, criteria for eligibility for the service, staff code of conduct, induction and training programme, and the appraisal system and its review. Also included were less formal documents, such as notes to and from staff, appraisal outcomes (protecting confidentiality), correspondence with trainers and consultants, and so on, demonstrating that this was not merely a paper exercise, but that the achievement of the targets was (and remains) part of the everyday work of the organization.

Following recognition, IIP employers are reviewed every 3 years to ensure that they are maintaining the standard. The organization referred to here was fortunate to receive substantial financial support from its local TEC in paying for consultancy support. Small organizations probably need such help, if collecting and presenting evidence, and maintaining supervision of progress, is not to become too onerous for staff. Larger organizations will appoint their own internal IIP lead officer, often a senior member of a personnel department, to undertake this role. Organizations that have achieved recognition find that it 'unites the whole staff with a common goal'; that 'it puts the organization in the news'; that 'it really made me stop and think – to question what I was doing and why'.

There are a number of advantages arising out of commitment to Investors in People. First, the exercise requires the management and staff of the organization to focus on the critical role of *all* the staff in delivering a quality service. The role of training and development – both in understanding the organization's aims and objectives, and in developing specific skills as needed – is subject to rigorous review and evaluation. IIP encourages the organization to develop a procedure for identifying training needs, and evaluating the results of training, in a systematic way.

Second, the exercise brings staff together for a common purpose. The sense of disparateness that is bound to invade the kind of organization that employs large numbers of part-time staff on out-placements, as so many caring organizations do, can be challenged by a new sense of collegiality and commitment; and the achievement of IIP recognition brings a heightened sense of self-esteem.

Third, other agencies, particularly funding agencies, will look upon an organization's work with a renewed respect, once they learn that they are committed to IIP. It has perhaps been inevitable that statutory providers have in the past looked upon the voluntary sector as, at worst, well-meaning amateurs in the provision of services. The new arrangements for provision make this attitude unacceptable, but it may take a long time for perceptions to change.

Recognition also enhances an organization's standing in the business and training networks of the area. The number of organizations gaining recognition nationally passed 1000 in December 1994. Admission to this fairly exclusive 'club' can bring contact with local businesses dealing with a wide range of goods and services. This has already resulted in some innovative thinking. For example, if a voluntary organization can provide a short-term caring service for the public sector alongside public and private providers, why should it not equally do so in the private sector? What sort of care might be needed by private purchasers who can afford to pay commercial rates, and therefore subsidize the public provision, maintain the organization's levels of demand, and perhaps turn part-time employees into full-timers? All employers face costs incurred by 'caring issues'. Staff who are late, miss days at work, are unable to give extra time to urgent jobs, or find it difficult to concentrate on their work, because they have older or disabled relatives or children to care for, have a substantial if as yet unmeasured impact on their places of employment. A contract with a voluntary organization to provide short-term and/or emergency care can make life much easier for a company of any size.

Finally, the benefits of 'tidying up' the procedures and policies that an organization accumulates cannot be overestimated. Managers in the voluntary sector, as we have seen in earlier chapters, can feel overwhelmed by the structural long-term needs of an organization, alongside a reluctance to abandon the everyday short-term needs of administration and service provision. The opportunity that IIP offers to sort out, update and prioritize, is invaluable after a period of rapid change and growth. It helps to put management 'back in charge', assists in identifying shifting priorities and, generally, puts people back on task.

Naturally, IIP can consume enormous amounts of time, money and paperwork. The key questions to ask at the outset are: Would we/should we be doing (most of) this anyway? What benefits will there be for the organization *apart from* the ultimate recognition? If these questions can be answered positively, and the resources of money and personnel can be found, commitment is justified. The statement of evidence for each indicator as given by one voluntary organization is shown in Table 6.2.

Table 6.2 Investors in People statement of evidence

Indicator	*Issue*
1 Commitment	
1.1 There is a public commitment from the most senior level within the organization to develop people	Stated in the handbook; reaffirmed at training groups (monthly) and other workshops, through the induction and training programme, and through the appraisal system. Confirmed by questionnaire responses
1.2 Employees at all levels are aware of the broad aims or vision of the organization	The original training programme involved staff in the formulation of these, which are reviewed on a regular basis in training groups. Induction and training programmes confirm the mission statement with new staff (which has recently been reworded by staff). Confirmed by questionnaire responses
1.3 There is a written but flexible plan which sets out business goals and targets	Service objectives have been in place for 18 months. The need for a business plan was recognized by the management committee in 1994, and has now been prepared and approved. This sets out priorities and development objectives
1.4 The plan identifies broad development needs and specifies how they will be assessed and met	The business plan identifies areas of development and priorities agreed by the management committee. Evaluations prepared by the project consultant address these, in the form of quality standards and objectives

Table 6.2 Cont'd

Indicator	*Issue*
1.5 The employer has considered what employees at all levels will contribute to the success of the organization and has communicated this effectively to them	Management staff prepare training programmes in consultation with staff, which are evaluated and reviewed by all staff and consultants. Questionnaire responses demonstrate a high degree of understanding and commitment of staff. Staff demonstrate in interview (see evaluations), and in training and appraisal, their understanding of the centrality of their role in the delivery of the organization's services
1.6 (if applicable) Management communicates with employee representatives a vision of where the organization is going and the contribution employees (and their representatives) will make to its success	Care workers are represented on the management committee, which addresses all strategic management issues in its meetings and in its own training programme
2 Planning	
2.1 The written plan identifies the resources that will be used to meet training and development needs	The annual budget identifies an amount set aside for training and for project consultancy, including evaluation
2.2 Training and development needs are regularly reviewed against business objectives	Evaluations perform a regular function of measuring organizational needs against organizational objectives
2.3 A process exists for regularly reviewing the training and development needs of all employees	Monthly training groups and annual appraisal offer group and individual opportunities for reviewing training and development needs, in addition to the regular accessibility of management staff
2.4 Responsibility for developing people is clearly identified throughout the organization, starting at the top	The management committee, management staff and care workers are acquainted with the organizational structure and responsibilities on induction, which is reaffirmed through groups
2.5 Managers are competent to carry out their responsibilities for developing people	Evaluation and the management training programme offer opportunities for management staff to review their own competencies
2.6 Targets and standards are set for development actions	The project's quality standards and management objectives are clear statements derived from the mission statement against which performance is evaluated and development actions formulated
2.7 Where appropriate, training targets are linked to external standards, and particularly to NVQs and Units	Appraisals allow opportunities for staff to express their aspirations for external qualifications. The project coordinator is an assessor in NVQ (Care), and a number of staff have achieved Level 3
3 Action	
3.1 All new employees are	The induction and training programme, and

Table 6.2 Cont'd

Indicator	*Issue*
introduced effectively to the organization and are given the training and development they need to do their jobs	support offered through mentoring, to newly appointed staff
3.2 The skills of existing employees are developed in line with business objectives	Business plan objectives (v) and (vi) emphasize the centrality of quality service delivery, towards which all training is directed
3.3 All employees are made aware of the development opportunities open to them	The induction and training programme, training groups and appraisal are arenas in which training opportunities are discussed and offered
3.4 All employees are encouraged to help identify and meet their job-related development needs	Again, training groups are the principal vehicles for this, alongside the availability of management staff and formal appraisal
3.5 Effective action takes place to achieve the training and development objectives of individuals and the organization	The training groups and programmes are evaluated by participants and by the project consultant
3.6 Managers are actively involved in supporting employees to meet their training and development needs	Training groups are coordinated by management staff, and the agenda formulated jointly by them with the staff. The management committee is involved in the appraisal programme
4 Evaluation	
4.1 The organization evaluates how its development of people is contributing to business goals and targets	The appraisal system has been reviewed in the year since its inception; regular external evaluations are conducted against explicit standards by the team from the Policy Studies Institute and the project consultant
4.2 The organization evaluates whether its development actions have achieved its objectives	Evaluations against quality standards are conducted by project consultants and considered by the management committee. The management committee holds regular workshop sessions with the project consultant
4.3 The outcomes of training and development are evaluated at individual, team and organizational levels	By management committee, management staff and care workers in training groups, and through appraisal
4.4 Top management understand the broad costs and benefits of developing people	Questionnaire responses reveal this
4.5 The continuing commitment of top management to developing people is communicated to all employees	The project handbook affirms the actions of management

Investors in People has been criticized for the absence of any explicit references to equality of opportunity in its material. Indeed, some of the training of advisers and assessors which took place before 1994, when only a small number of companies were accredited as trainers, was open to criticism on these grounds. Earlier in that year, one group of potential assessors was told that, in constructing a sample of employees for interview, they should ensure a spread of age, experience, length of service and position within the hierarchy. Gender, disability and ethnic origin were not mentioned as variables. When this was questioned, it was suggested that a spread of ethnic origin could be obtained by 'looking down the staff list and picking out any ethnic names – for example, anyone called Mackintosh would probably be Scottish'! This kind of reasoning gave a justifiably bad name to some of the preparation of advisers and assessors. In March 1994, the Commission for Racial Equality published a draft document, *TECs, LECs and Racial Equality*. This comprised a recommended checklist of Investors in People indicators for equal opportunity. The guidance material for IIP had already made it clear, though not prominently so, that

> All organisations which are recognized as Investors in People are expected to comply with the legislation concerning sex and race discrimination, and to meet the requirements of legislation on the employment of people with disabilities. Commitment to equality of opportunity and action to secure it are a part of improving the performance of all employees. Therefore references to 'all staff' should be read to mean 'all staff, regardless of race, gender, marital status or disability'.
>
> (CRE 1994)

The CRE document also points out that:

> There is a close link between equal opportunity and developing people to achieve effective business performance. This is because equal opportunity measures include:
>
> Finding ways of realising the talents of those who have been held back due to discrimination or past disadvantage.
>
> Applying fair and relevant selection criteria.
>
> Removing unjustifiable barriers to effective performance and opportunities to develop skills and abilities.
>
> The need for these is reflected in the Investors in People Indicators.

The document then goes on to identify some key points to be addressed under each of the IIP headings: Commitment, Planning, Action and Evaluation. While IIP UK did not take up the recommendations of the CRE, any organization can, of course, activate these as a 'value-added' element to their commitment.

In implementing any quality initiatives, it is vital to appreciate that quality implies equality: equality of opportunity for users and staff is an indispensable criterion of a quality approach. If *all* users and staff are not offered the same quality service and support, the organization cannot claim to have absorbed the meaning of the term.

THE FUTURE OF THE VOLUNTARY SECTOR

- Internal threats to change
- External threats to change
- Benefits of the voluntary sector
- Key components of change
- Empowering the voluntary sector

Organizations and individuals have to study change if they are to deal with it. There are, inevitably, some features that change brings which are inherently dangerous to the health of an organization, just as it is now recognized that change itself can affect the mental and physical health of an individual. Let us now examine both the internal and external threats to change.

Internal threats to change

Nostalgia for a 'golden age'. The creation and early life of a voluntary organization is an exciting if exhausting period for those involved. Creativity is a key element, considerable learning takes place, new contacts are made and new ideas are generated. The founders of the organization will be carried along on a wave of enthusiasm; all the features of collegiality, the sense of shared purpose, the endless commitment of time and energy – so hard to create and maintain in a mature organization – will flourish without apparent effort. As the organization grows, and new people are recruited, and as processes become more bureaucratic and complicated, the founders of the organization are likely to protect their own 'pure' vision, and to develop a sense of superiority over newcomers. These feelings can manifest themselves in the day-to-day work of the organization, and perhaps in particular in policy and decision-making forums. They can, therefore, get in the way of development and growth, making newcomers feel intrusive, especially when they hear people saying, 'Wasn't it great when . . .'. The organization's vision has to be protected, but it is important that the vision should be interpreted through the quality and quantity of the service delivered, not through the methods or personnel of the organization.

Special knowledge held by 'the old guard'. This is closely connected to the nostalgia syndrome. In order to protect their privileged positions, founders may – consciously or unconsciously – not pass on the understanding of the processes and the personalities of the local community, and of local government, which have been crucial to the organization's success. This is particularly dangerous where senior staff are recruited over the heads of existing staff, and staff may seek to protect some of their authority by keeping to themselves vital knowledge. The games that can be played include hiding information and showing exaggerated or inappropriate familiarity with management committee members and other comparatively senior figures. One way to offset the worst effects of this tendency is to put experienced workers in charge of inducting and training new staff, through the kinds of training and support groups with which teams in SSDs are familiar. By recognizing *explicitly* rather than merely implicitly that the performance of new staff depends upon the support of the existing team, the latter is given *formal* responsibility for the performance of the organization. Support teams reinforce the mission and develop responsibility, ownership and commitment.

Loss of focus on the mission. Missions and priorities within missions do change, and among a growing staff focus can shift or be lost, both intentionally and otherwise. That is why it is so important that the sharing of aims and objectives among all staff and volunteers happens on a regular basis. The annual group event – perhaps linked to the annual general meeting, perhaps effectively replacing that otherwise, sometimes barren occasion – is an opportunity to do this. Structures such as support groups, in place throughout the year, allow continuous communication among and between workers and volunteers.

The organization can become a scapegoat (for workers) or a 'dumping ground' (for users). When change is unplanned, unnegotiated or unmanaged, the resulting tensions can cause resentment – and sometimes sheer exhaustion – which spills over into private lives, and which can be blamed solely on the workplace or on the provider of services. It is therefore important to identify the causes of stress, to recognize it in a comprehensive health and safety policy and to encourage people to talk about failures and frustrations, as well as to celebrate success. Similarly, change in the workplace can become a vehicle for staff: either of success, where employees pin their current feelings of worth and their future careers on the outcomes of change, or of failure, where employees blame their own frustrations and lack of self-esteem on the organization. Both are dangerous. This issue should be addressed by developing more effective communication throughout the organization. In order to reduce the stress of day-to-day contact with users in severe need, arrangements can be made for regular closure of the office to callers (with back-up contact systems, of course), extra care can be taken in the allocation of work (and care workers who want to take on extra loads can be discouraged), and a training strategy must be developed (see Chapter 6). In relations with clients, the eligibility criteria should be codified, so that staff have formal organizational support in saying 'No' and 'No more'. Systems can be 'firmed up', giving less room for open-ended decision-making in routine cases; and the situation should be explained to purchasers, in the hope of avoiding inappropriate referrals. Taken together, these steps might be seen as the 'bureaucratization' of the organization, moving towards the stereotypical inflexibility of the statutory sector. The quality components discussed in the previous chapter act as safeguards to ensure this cannot happen.

Systems become strained or collapse. This is an obvious corollary of expansion, let alone of change. This makes the annual review of procedures suggested above and the regular reassessment of management objectives essential.

Accommodation becomes inadequate. And the philosophy of 'make do and mend' comes into play. Again, regular reviews of organizational need, including assessments of need by all staff, help to focus on solving problems, rather than living with them.

Getting sufficient skills in place in time, and mobilizing and directing them. An anxiety not to overstaff, or overload a management committee, leads to the opposite, creating a permanent sense of strained resources. Again, regular assessment of organizational need, preferably within a 3–5 year staff development plan, can avoid this. Organizations need to have to hand an 'ideal' staffing structure which they would implement given a clean sheet. While this almost always remains only an ideal towards which to strive, it does focus on need rather than merely replacing vacant posts in a flurry of urgency.

The staff and committee of an organization need to look at themselves at least on an annual basis in order to assess what *has changed* and what *is likely to change*. This exercise enables planning. One organization completed such an exercise, in the middle of a period of rapid growth. The results were as shown in Table 7.1.

This type of review enables the organization to devise a list of opportunities, or anticipated changes, at all levels. It can be seen from point 14 in the left-hand column of Table 7.1 that the stylization of organizations within community care as male/female arose (see Table 5.1). This model came to have great significance for a small organization facing 'the big league'. The stylization arose through the metaphors adopted by the participants in a workshop focusing on change. Table 7.2 is developed from an exercise in which members of the staff and the management committee first characterized what they meant when they used a succession of gender-based metaphors. Following a discussion of the meanings, they then prepared a series of 'declarations' which recognized the acceptable changes implied by growth and 'professionalization', and firmly rejected a set of characteristics which seemed to be, but would not be accepted as, consequences. These can be synthesized into a series of declarations (see Table 7.3).

The external threats are largely structural. To what extent can the voluntary sector, in its changing relationships with funding agencies, retain the support of the public? The funding of contract work, as we have seen, is largely historical, based on the comparatively niggardly sums provided in grant-aid. Purchasing agencies fund on the assumptions of:

- Little or no staff training provided by the organization independent of the purchaser.
- Cheap or free premises provided by the organization or the purchaser.
- Low rates of pay, or secondment.

Table 7.1 An exercise in perceptions of change

What has changed	*What will change*
1 From 4 to 900 hours a week of service delivered	1 Central government funding finishes next year
2 Number of care workers doubled	2 Assistant manager to leave next year
3 New assistant manager post	3 Administration hours must increase
4 New chair and vice-chairs	4 Status of the organization to change to a limited company
5 Users have more severe needs	5 Working on contracts, not grants
6 More night-time usages	6 Will contracts dictate and monitor the quality of the service?
7 Funds to work with more elderly mentally ill clients	7 Committee roles will change
8 Accountability has intensified and must fit into complex networks	8 An invasion by 'big services' seems dangerous
9 Staff have developed – they're more focused and more self-aware	
10 The need for the service is more clearly identified	
11 Other agencies have other, conflicting agendas	
12 There's a growth in the community's understanding of community care	
13 Inter-dependence with other services creates stresses; they have other priorities	
14 'Little' organizations are isolated, while the 'big boys' are macho male-dominated agencies	
15 A standby system for night-time cover	
16 More Asian people involved with the project	

Table 7.2 Organizational stereotypes

Female	*Male*
Accept	Control
Remain static	Develop
Understand	Discover new markets
Receive money	Negotiate
Support	Have structures
Include	Shut out
Say 'yes' or 'maybe'	Say 'no' clearly
Are flexible	Are rigid/firm
Expect failure (or requires lower odds against success)	Expect success
Do things/organize things	Produce things
See routes as destination	See destinations as routes

Table 7.3

We will	*We will not*
Say 'no' clearly	Remain static
Be flexible	Accept other people's rules wholesale
Expect success	Be intimidated
Set appropriate and achievable targets	Be controlled
Negotiate	Be destructive
Minimize our vulnerability	Be aggressive
Value our own integrity, ability and dignity	Challenge unreasonably
Question	
Avoid dogmatism and celebrate diversity	
Produce things and organize things	
See problems *and* solutions	

- Assumptions of a comparatively low-level service sustained by goodwill and accepted with tolerance by a public unused to quality provision.

The suspicion that this was so was reinforced by the publication of a joint report by the National Council for Voluntary Organizations and the Association of Directors of Social Services (NCVO/ADSS 1995). In this report, Scope is one of a number of charities claiming that its contracts with local authorities have been underfunded by up to 10 per cent. The document recommends that local councils should separate grant-giving from contracting, and ensure that 'the cost of (local authority) services should be provided from publicly provided funds':

> Where consistent with its charitable objects and charity law, a VO [voluntary organization] may decide to draw on its charitable income, for example, to provide an additional or better service than the purchaser specifies . . . [Local authorities] should not assume that VOs generally will be willing or able regularly to make good perceived inadequacies in public funds or otherwise relieve the public purse.

This is, of course, easier to write than to do. Quantifying the exact level of service, and matching it to a cost, is a more complex business than this implies.

It is this tension that could result in alienating the public from the voluntary sector. As has been suggested above, one of the weaknesses in evaluating services provided by the voluntary sector is the gratitude factor. It is the simultaneous duty of the provider to create and meet ever growing expectations, and therefore to face the inevitable backlash of greater demand for greater quality. Service quality tends to preclude a cosy relationship between supplier and user.

Meanwhile, local government itself remains under attack. Although some of the more recent assaults on its autonomy have been repulsed, it remains a sector which has seen its power to act, and to finance itself, independently whittled away. Faced with competition from, and participation in, the market of provision of community care, the tensions have produced a confusion of aims. Public service providers have been ill-equipped to deal in the market, when their primary focus has been on inclusiveness. The market is not required to cover the whole population, as the welfare system and charities must be prepared to do – only those whose purchasing power gives them the right of entry:

> Markets can produce perverse results. There is an inbuilt tendency to cherry-pick. Social functions are executed poorly. Short-termism becomes endemic. Markets are not value free. Passengers, viewers and patients all become homogenised as 'customers' and 'clients' who consume 'products'. But the importance of customers is that they spend; the capacity to be a citizen depends upon spending power, without which citizenship disappears.
>
> (Hutton 1995: 217–18)

Once again, the voluntary sector slips into an uneasy gap between the public and the private. Are we entitled to the services of the voluntary sector? Or are they a privilege? Charity, in the pejorative sense of the word? What are the implications for workers and volunteers in the voluntary sector if the services they provide are now public rights? Is this changing the way voluntary organizations operate, for better or for worse? It is, perhaps, the insistence by users upon their rights which causes the most personal distress in the direct delivery of a service. It is the users, and their responses, who are the subject of most staff room conversations in day centres and domiciliary care. The difficult patient, the awkward customer and the troublesome carer are legend, but have to be dealt with every day. In the public sector, the service *has* to be provided, and the users know that – so we have grilles in job centres and housing offices. In the private sector, perhaps the customer is always right – but if not, the customer can go elsewhere. The voluntary sector admits the tensions of both approaches – with the exclusivity of the private sector and the personal commitment and rhetoric of public service:

> What is once again at work is Britain's weak tradition of citizenship combining with the tradition's mirror image – the celebration of the private. It all adds subtly to the processes of social exclusion . . . The already marginalised and disaffected become more marginalised still.
>
> (Hutton 1995: 219)

This book has focused on what the voluntary sector can do for its clients, and on the particular characteristics it has for delivering best quality services. But it would be wrong not to consider what voluntary organizations do for the people who manage them and work for them. Mike Hudson (1995) has summarized the size and impact of the voluntary sector on our lives. Using figures produced by NCVO in 1993, he estimates a total of 170,000 charities in the UK, excluding churches, clubs, sports organizations and unregistered bodies. This probably amounts to over 500,000 organizations, with some 13 million people involved in volunteering activities every month – half the adult population.

Voluntary organizations offer a wide variety of work experience to their staff. Much voluntary work, both administrative and practical particularly in times of recession, is undertaken with a view to developing the volunteer's curriculum vitae. There is also much valuable experience to be gained from serving on a management committee or board. The range of management tasks undertaken, from strategic management to financial administration, offers a type of experience which it can take years to gain through a job. The business sector has yet to latch on, in a significant way, to the benefits which their employees can gain in terms of management training off the job. It has been more common to use the voluntary sector as a pasture for experienced executives who may have come near the end of their useful lives within a company. Whether this sums up the private sector's view of the voluntary sector is unclear. But sponsorship can take many forms, and need not be directly financial. A commitment of time from rising employees in any sphere of work can pay dividends to the sponsor, and be a comparatively cheap and very effective training method.

Working with organizations can raise both the self-esteem and public esteem of volunteers. As Hudson (1995: 37) writes:

> They join governing boards, particularly of larger and more prestigious organizations, because of the recognition, esteem and status that is attached to board membership. Such membership frequently leads to contacts with other people in powerful positions, to increased influence and a greater sense of self-worth.

Volunteers use volunteering as a social activity. We know from research into adult education classes that interest in the subject to be studied is only one – and may not be the primary – factor in attendance. Studying class lists from year to year reveals that many students attend time and time again, studying Spanish one year, Continental Cookery the next year, Archaeology in a third. Sometimes it seems that the other people attending form the basis for the choice, sometimes merely the night on which the course takes place. But it is clear that the social factor is at least as important as any other. So, too, it is with volunteering. Just as Tony Hancock (in 'The Blood Donor') decided not to join the Young Conservatives because he couldn't play table-tennis and wasn't looking for a wife, so our choices of community involvement revolve around a complex network of motivations. Who else goes and whether it is fun or not may be the most simplistic reasons, and are therefore as likely to be as true as any.

Working in, or volunteering with, the voluntary sector does provide an outlet for those who want to spend their working lives in an ideology of public service. Nor should we underestimate just what a contribution the 13 million or so volunteers do make. People may be coy about admitting it, but the social fabric of the country would collapse without the meals-on-wheels, the lifeboats, the hostels for the homeless, the support groups for disabled people, and the leisure and sports clubs. Volunteering is a genuine community service, usually undertaken because people feel that they should put something back. It is true, albeit a cliché.

Volunteering is a way into the management of the community structures that influence our lives. It is easily forgotten by those whose lives are spent in politicking and lobbying, in meetings and networking, that to many (perhaps most), the way things get done in this country is a mystery.

Community figures are likely to be people who have worked out how to get things done, and obtained access to the funds and support that politics offers. But ask the average person in the street which agency collects their rubbish, which is responsible for their street lighting, which runs the buses and which gives advice to citizens, and they will not know. The complex and fragmented jigsaw of public services – now much privatized and even more piecemeal – serves to distance ordinary people from the way in which their lives are run. We have a dependency culture, not because some people (some 30 per cent, according to Hutton) are likely to be dependent on benefit for most of their lives, or because others (another 30 per cent) have very unpredictable incomes, but because the systems that govern our lives are so remote. The anomie that is created by having services delivered by remote local or national authorities, through departmental, arms-length or independent agencies, leaves people bewildered and apparently apathetic. In the early 1940s, the editor of a local paper in Tennessee reviewed the impact of the Tennessee Valley Authority dam project on his community: 'The most significant advance', he wrote, 'has been made in the thinking of a people. They are no longer afraid. *They have caught the vision of their own powers*' (quoted in Lilienthal 1944; my italics). The consumerist approach is essentially weak because it encourages dependency, fails to empower the consumer and embrace wider objectives such as the strengthening of local democracy. We need to see the public as *simultaneously* users and providers. Such an approach does not aim to strengthen local democracy *per se*, nor to empower the consumer. Rather, it seeks to redefine the relationship between local government and the public, confirming that local government is one – and only one – element of community democracy, and that the public are not so much consumers of local services, but the fundamental element that makes up a liberal community democracy.

A radical approach such as this does not attempt to abolish power – an attempt that brought about the downfall of many radical and anarchist voluntary organizations in the 1970s – but provides the channel through which people can approach power and develop the personal resources to use it:

> If an organization enables people to articulate and meet their needs free from domination, and if it does so without contravening other people's needs and rights, then it should be seen as a positive gain . . . Democracy is a dynamic, and it doesn't consist of a static set of tricks . . . Users choose to have their children in certain hospitals because those hospitals are more open-minded about new birthing methods, or they send their children to particular schools because they are happier with the education provided there. All these choices which will be made within the public sector . . . might be described as simply the luxury of the well-informed middle-class. But surely the aim must be to expand the availability of this 'luxury' so that the widest possible range of users – instead of being progressively alienated from the services provided by the public sector – take an active part in saying rather loudly what they want. Only then will public services become more responsive to people's felt needs.
>
> (Landry *et al.* 1985: 80, 85, 91)

It is this role that the voluntary sector can fulfil, if it takes its duties seriously. If it fails, it will become effectively another branch of the increasingly beleaguered public sector. If it takes the consumerist path, it will merely be another, barely distinguishable, feature of private provision.

One anecdotal but nonetheless powerful pattern has emerged via work with groups for preschool children. On many occasions, in rural, inner-city or peripheral housing estates with predominantly rented property, on local action committees, on school governing bodies and on community centre boards, there will be a young woman, with small children, who has left school at the earliest possible age and with the minimum of qualifications. The path to community participation usually starts with the parents and toddlers group, and the playgroup. Playgroups need committees to affiliate to the PreSchool Playgroups Association, and it is often a struggle to recruit, especially where community attachment is weak and self-confidence low. The mother is inveigled on, and after a year or so, there is a vacancy for a secretary or treasurer. She is persuaded. Next year, she becomes the chair. When the youngest child leaves for playgroup, she follows on to that committee. She now has a reputation as someone who can be relied on, perhaps someone who gets things done. The infant school headteacher hears of this, and she is asked to join the Parent Teachers Association – and soon, the governing body. Now she is getting accustomed to the ways in which power operates, to learn the language of committees, and to have an idea of how things can be changed – slowly but effectively. She may return to school, or attend adult education classes, to try to gain some of the qualifications she failed at school. Now she is part of the community network. If there is an action committee, a local neighbourhood group, a community event, she will be invited. She may start studying through the Open University, or attend a local college. (Often, by this time, she will have outgrown her partner, and be looking after the children alone.) By a gradual immersion in the systems which allow participation, she has caught the vision of her own powers.

Those of us working with community groups will have heard this kind of story a number of times. It is a profile of emancipation, but it is hard work, and it may not feel very rewarding. But it is the kind of profile that changes communities and the people who live in them. They are the people who run Beavers and Rainbows, who organize summer play schemes for the children, and harry the local council for sports facilities, or for street lighting where women are afraid to walk at night. Sometimes their campaigns are so successful that they are recruited, formally or informally, on to the lists of recognized community workers. Sometimes local residents refer to them as 'Not one of us – one of them'. But such people are the core of organic communities and embody people's capacity to run their own lives. It is a far cry from the establishment model of advancement. In February 1995, the *Guardian* reported on the previous day's hearing of the Nolan Committee on standards in public life. The committee was hearing from the Dixons Group chairman and Conservative Party donor, Stanley Kalms, on his appointment to the Funding Agency for Schools, a body with a £2 billion budget for distribution to grant-maintained schools:

> He [Kalms] subsequently got the job, but said yesterday he would not serve on quangos if he was required to apply formally and be interviewed for a vacancy, as the Government recommended earlier this week. Mr Kalms, chairman of the Kings Hospital Trust and a member of the Funding Agency for Schools, told the Nolan Committee on standards in public life: 'I heard the Funding Agency was being formed. I indicated to people that walked the corridors that it was an area that I ought to be involved in'. He said 'the people that walked the corridors' was a minister. He and other private sector businessmen 'bring fresh air, fresh thought, fresh challenge to the quango movement. It would be a sad loss if the barriers of entry were too high to get over. I would not apply to an advert. If we have to publicly apply, I think you will lose us because it is not the process by which we are used to getting appointments.'
>
> (*Guardian*, 16 February 1995)

In a radical model, which nurtures individuals, which seeks to give voice to people in what Paulo Freire calls 'the culture of silence' (1972), members of the community are seen as:

- Responsible for the direction, content and quality of services used by them and their families.
- Committed in the long term to the community, and having a complex set of relationships with it.
- Acting in the interests of others as well as of themselves.
- Proactive, i.e. initiating change, rather than merely reacting to change about them.
- Likely to develop a substantial rationality, or an understanding of their relationship with the world, through a measure of control and a capacity for individual growth.

Five key components for the changing organization

Let us return to those five key areas noted in Chapter 1. These are the key components of change which an organization must address, to operate effectively in what has been called a 'post-entrepreneurial' society:

The management

The volunteer committee and the staff must welcome change. Change must be seen as a way of life, an inevitable and desirable state of things for an organic organization. Personnel must never be content with things as they are, but only with a constantly improving service.

Quality

The quality of service must be a recognizable and realizable goal. There must be continuous self-assessment and continuous measurement. Targets must be reviewed as soon as they become realizable, but there must be plenty of

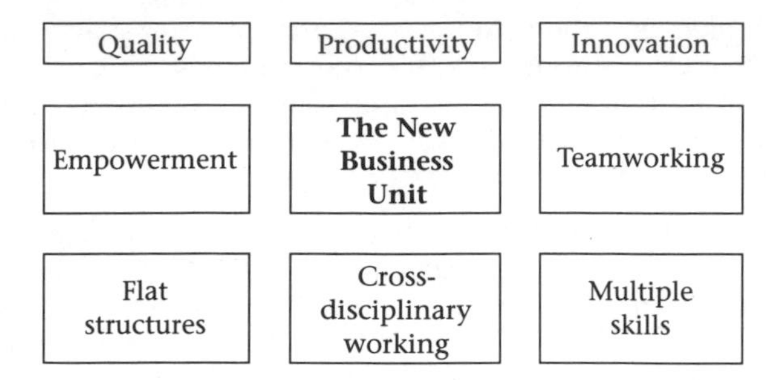

Figure 7.1 The New Business Unit

opportunity to celebrate the quality that is achieved. Quality must be a daily target for all.

Policies and procedures

There must be a reliable system of operation, represented by a portfolio of organization documents, which is negotiated, regularly reviewed and communicated, and which becomes the handbook by which personnel operate.

The post-entrepreneurial unit

Successful business units will run shared facilities to gain economies of scale; will facilitate, retain and develop a larger pool of management competence and expertise – where necessary by buying out; will coordinate and facilitate networking and information exchange; will plan strategically, 'scanning the horizon'; and will provide common values and a shared purpose (see Fig. 7.1).

Federation

The organization should look out for innovative relationships with a disparate variety of businesses in all sectors.

Empowering the voluntary sector

The voluntary sector is 'a good thing'. It delivers a wide variety of services, some of which are not delivered elsewhere, some of which are delivered more appropriately than elsewhere. It has a unique capacity to absorb change quickly, to experiment and to innovate. Millions of people use it as an outlet for their need to contribute to the community around them. It is a way in which people can affirm their social identity, and a vehicle through which they can learn about the ways in which society works, and in which they can experience their own personal growth. It gives a structure and a sense of purpose to millions of people. And it is no longer taken for granted. It cannot be ignored that the voluntary sector is a major player in the provision of social services throughout the country.

But it is still under-resourced and undervalued. What steps can be taken to ensure that the voluntary sector is given the support it needs to provide a democratic quality service in areas of social need?

Funding – obviously. The ≥10 per cent calculated as the shortfall on contracts needs to be replaced. This calculation at least gives a rough figure to which to work. Charges for services should be calculated on actual costs, *including* essential training, quality premises, and so on.

Devolution of decision-making. The powers that have been whittled away from local authorities must be restored, i.e. powers of fund-raising and decision-making. Decisions on services must be made at the most local level possible. Neighbourhood and community action groups, supported by local councils, but with local people predominating, should be distributing the money available for the voluntary sector. This may imply a movement towards regional government.

Funding specifically for the training of volunteers. A National Training Council, perhaps administered by a confederation of organizations such as the Directory for Social Change, the National Council for Voluntary Organizations, the National Association of Councils for Voluntary Service, Action for Governor Information and Training, should provide free or subsidized training for voluntary roles in the public and voluntary sectors, such as trustees, management committee and board members, members of health authorities and school governing bodies. Training would not be compulsory nationally, but purchasers and other funders might, on a local basis, require registered organizations to have trained management volunteers. The funding necessary for this would only be a small token of the enormous contribution made by volunteers to the national infrastructure.

A study of how communities work, and of the opportunities they offer people to participate. A true Citizen's Charter would be a set of rights and entitlements by which all residents can become involved in community decision-making.

Such measures would further empower the voluntary sector and the people who work in it, would help them to manage the changes that are happening within their organizations, as well as the changes in societal structures that impact upon them, and would more deeply entrench within our communities the indispensable contribution they make to all our lives.

BIBLIOGRAPHY

Adirondack, S. (1990) *Getting Ready for Contracts*. London: Directory of Social Change.
Belbin, R. (1981) *Management Teams*. London: Heinemann.
Callaghan, J. (1992) *Costing for Contracts*. London: National Council for Voluntary Organizations/Directory of Social Change.
Charity Commissioners (1993) *Responsibilities of Charity Trustees*. London: Charity Commission.
Commission for Racial Equality (1994) *TECs, LECs and Racial Equality*. London: CRE.
Crosby, P. (1979) *Quality is Free*. New York: Mentor Books.
Crosland, A. (1956) *The Future of Socialism*. London: Cape.
Deming, W. (1986) *Out of the Crisis*. Cambridge: Cambridge University Press.
Department of Health (1989) *Caring for People: Community Care in the Next Decade and Beyond*. London: HMSO.
Department of Health (1993) *Caring for People Who Live at Home*. News-sheet No. 1, Spring 1993.
Department of Health (1994) *A Framework for Local Community Care Charters in England*. London: HMSO.
Department of Health and Social Security (1990) *Inspecting Home Care Services*. Social Services Inspectorate. London: HMSO.
Department of Health and Social Services Inspectorate (1990) *Caring for Quality: Inspecting Home Care Services. A guide to the SSI Method*. London: HMSO.
Drucker, P. (1985) *Innovation and Entrepreneurship*. London: Heinemann.
Duane, M. (1991) *Work, Language and Education in the Industrial State*. London: Freedom Press.
Fletcher, C. (1984) Adult education and community needs: Towards a distinctive extramural contribution. In P. Widlake (ed.), *Evaluation Report No. 2: A First Guide to Needs Assessment*. Coventry: Community Education Development Centre.
Foucault, M. (1976) Disciplinary power and subjection. In S. Lukes (ed.), *Power*. Oxford: Blackwell.
Freire, P. (1972) *Pedagogy of the Oppressed*. London: Penguin.
Gaventa, J. (1980) *Power and Powerlessness: Quiescence and Rebellion in an Appalachian Valley*. Chicago, IL: University of Chicago Press.
Green, D. (1981) *Power and Party in an English City: An Account of Single-Party Rule*. London: Allen and Unwin.
Griffiths, R. (1988) *Community Care: Agenda for Action*. London: HMSO.
Handy, C. (1988) *Understanding Voluntary Organizations*. Harmondsworth: Penguin.

Harris, M. (1984) Management committees in voluntary agencies. In B. Knight (ed.), *Management in Voluntary Organisations*. London: Association of Researchers in Voluntary Action and Community Involvement.
Hawtin, M. *et al.* (1994) *Community Profiling: Auditing Social Needs*. Buckingham: Open University Press.
Herzberg, F. (1966) *Work and the Nature of Man*. Cleveland, OH: Cleveland Publishing Company.
Hudson, M. (1995) *Managing Without Profit*. Harmondsworth: Penguin.
Hutton, W. (1995) *The State We're In*. London: Random House.
Kanter, R. (1983) *The Change Masters*. London: Counterpoint Unwin.
Landry, C. *et al.* (1985) *What a Way to Run a Railroad: An Analysis of Radical Failure*. London: Comedia Publishing Group.
Lawrie, A. (1995) *Managing Quality of Service*. London: Directory of Social Change.
Leat, D. (1993) *The Development of Community Care by the Independent Sector*. London: Policy Studies Institute.
Lilienthal, D. (1944) *TVA: Tennessee Valley Authority – Democracy on the March*. Harmondsworth: Penguin.
Lukes, C. (1974) *Power: A Radical View*. London: Macmillan.
Mill, J. S. (1982) *On Liberty*. Harmondsworth: Penguin.
National Council for Voluntary Organizations (1992) *On Trust*. Report of a Working Party on Trustee Training set up by NCVO and the Charity Commission. London: NCVO.
National Council for Voluntary Organizations/Association of Directors of Social Services (1995) *Community Care and Voluntary Organisations*. London: NCVO/ADSS.
Pestieau, J. (1993) *European Economy*, Issue No. 3. Brussels: European Commission.
Peters, T. (1987) *Thriving on Chaos*. London: Pan Books.
Sandwell Metropolitan Borough Council (1994) *Investing in Community*. Metropolitan Borough of Sandwell
Schattschneider, E. (1960) *The Semi-Sovereign People: A Realistic View of Democracy in America*. New York: Holt, Rinehart and Winston.
Schubert, W. (1990) Curriculum centralisation and decentralisation: Historical perspectives. Quoted in M. Bottery (1992) *The Ethics of Educational Management*. London: Cassell.
Schumpeter, J. (1942) *Capitalism, Socialism and Democracy*. New York: Harper and Row.
Taylor, F. (1911) *Principles of Scientific Management*. London: Harper and Row.
Terkel, S. (1972) *Working*. New York: Ballantine.
Toffler, A. (1970) *Future Shock*. London: Bodley Head.
Toffler, A. (1980) *The Third Wave*. London: Collins.
Thucydides (1970) Pericles' Funeral Speech, in *Greek Political Oratory*. Harmondsworth: Penguin.
Volunteer Centre UK (1990) *Voluntary Action Research*. Paper No. 1: Voluntary Activity: A Survey of Public Attitudes. London: Volunteer Centre UK.
Weir, S. and Hall, W. (1994) *Ego Trip: Extra-Governmental Organisations in the United Kingdom and their Accountability*. London: The Charter 88 Trust.
Williams, S. (1993) *Lloyds Bank Small Business Guide*. Harmondsworth: Penguin.
Wistow, G. *et al.* (1994) *Social Care in a Mixed Economy*. Buckingham: Open University Press.

APPENDIX A: A SAMPLE APPOINTMENTS PROCEDURE

This procedure is designed to appoint the best possible candidate to the post, regardless of irrelevant issues.

1 Identification of vacancies

1.1 When a vacancy is identified, the management board will decide what the vacancy is to be filled. In the case of replacement of a postholder, the board will analyse the tasks to be performed and anticipate any changes requiring different or additional skills.

1.2 The board will draw up a description, comprising:

- the policies of the organization, and the context in which the postholder will be expected to work;
- the title of the job;
- the main purpose of the job;
- the main tasks of the job, ranked in order of importance;
- the scope of the job;
- the lines of responsibility and accountability of the post;
- the hours required to be worked;
- the remuneration offered, according to experience and qualifications.

1.3 The job description will be couched in the most accessible language(s) possible.

2 Recruitment

2.1 The board will draw up a personnel specification identifying the attributes of the ideal candidate:

- *Physical make-up*: health, self-presentation and speech.
- *Attainments*: education, qualifications and experience.
- *General intelligence*: intellectual capacity.
- *Special aptitudes*: mechanical, manual dexterity, facility in use of words and figures.
- *Interests*: intellectual, practical, constructional, physically active, social, artistic.
- *Disposition*: acceptability, influence over others, steadiness, dependability, self-reliance.
- *Circumstances*: any special demands of the job, such as ability to work unsocial hours, drive, etc.

2.2 The person specification will be couched in the most accessible language(s) possible.
2.3 The board will draw up an advertisement to be placed in the national, local and ethnic press, and distributed to local community organizations and the Employment Service. The advertisement will specify the post to be filled, and the availability of application forms, job description and person specification. These will be available by telephone as well as written contact. The advertisement will also give a closing date at least 2 weeks from the last appearance of the advertisement and the expected dates of interview.
2.4 The advertisement will be couched in the most accessible language(s) possible.
2.5 The application form to be sent with the job details will invite only such information as is relevant to the post, and will be laid out in such a way that it is easily accessible to any potential applicants and helpful to the shortlisting panel in working to the job description and person specification. Candidates will be invited to attach a letter giving additional information if they wish.

3 Shortlisting

3.1 The management board will appoint one panel to undertake both shortlisting and interviewing, comprising at least one of its own members, the member of staff to be responsible for the postholder and, where possible, an existing member of staff with day-to-day knowledge of the job.
3.2 The panel will undertake to observe total confidentiality regarding the details of the applications.
3.3 The panel will reach agreement on the selection criteria based upon the job description and person specification, the weightings and interview questions. The selection panel will have to decide whether each requirement is *essential* or *desirable*. They will also have to decide whether the totality of requirements is realistic.
3.4 All applications received by the published closing date will be considered by the panel.
3.5 The panel will draw up a shortlist of candidates who fulfil the minimum selection criteria. Other applicants will be contacted, to thank them for their interest and inform them that they have not been shortlisted.
3.6 The panel will decide whether it is practicable to interview all shortlisted candidates and, if not, will agree the number of candidates to be interviewed and the list of those who appear most nearly to meet the person specification. Other applicants will be written to, to inform them that they have not been finally shortlisted at this time.
3.7 Shortlisted candidates will be contacted for invitation to interview and informed of the structure of the interview and the members of the panel.

4 Interviewing

4.1 All candidates will be introduced to all panel members and any observers, and informed at the beginning of their interview of the likely length and structure of the interview, and the means by which the final decision will be communicated.
4.2 The major part of each interview will comprise the same questions, based on the job description and person specification, asked by the same panel member. However, panel members may explore candidates' answers in greater depth, and may ask supplementary questions exploring relevant points raised in the form and letter of application.
4.3 The panel will use whatever weightings of the criteria have been agreed to reach their decision.

4.4 The panel will inform all candidates of the outcome at the earliest possible opportunity, and will offer debriefing to all unsuccessful candidates.
4.5 In the event of a failure to appoint, the panel will advise the management board of their intention, either to invite further candidates from the shortlist, or to readvertise the post in the same or different form.
4.6 The successful candidate will be appointed to the post as advertised and offered an induction procedure appropriate to the post.
4.7 The chair of the panel will collect all documents relating to the conduct of the appointment. All notes made throughout the proceedings by the panel members, together with one copy of each application, will be retained in a secure place for at least 6 months, in case of a challenge to the procedure. All other documents will be destroyed.

APPENDIX B: A SCHEME FOR MANAGEMENT COMMITTEE EVALUATION

	Yes	*No*	*Action*
Meetings			
1 Is notice of meetings delivered in good time?			
2 Is the agenda clear and supported by relevant documents?			
3 Is the purpose of each agenda item clear?			
4 Are all members treated equally?			
5 Are all members encouraged to speak?			
6 Are decisions clear, and is collective responsibility accepted?			
7 Is discussion kept to the point?			
8 Are all members punctual in attendance?			
9 Is the meeting room adequate and seating appropriate?			
10 Is everyone clear as to the action to be taken?			
Planning			
11 Is there a clear agreed organization development plan?			
12 Does the plan consider financial matters?			
13 Was the plan's preparation a cooperative effort with staff and members?			
14 Was the final form approved by the committee?			
15 Are all objectives clear and written down?			
16 Does the plan make clear what is to be done?			
17 Does the plan make clear who is responsible for each action?			

	Yes	*No*	*Action*
18 Does the plan make clear the start and finish dates for action?			
19 Does the plan include a system for monitoring and evaluating progress?			
20 Does the committee receive regular reports on progress, both internally and externally generated?			
Finance			
21 Is sufficient interest taken by all members in financial affairs?			
22 Do members understand their powers and responsibilities?			
23 Is lack of understanding treated sympathetically?			
24 Is there a clear statement of staff responsibilities?			
25 Is the budget monitored regularly?			
26 Do members receive regular reports on finances?			
27 Does the budget reflect organizational priorities?			
28 Is the budget part of longer-term financial planning?			
29 Do members understand their role in fundraising?			
30 Do members understand the long-term income trends?			
Employment			
31 Do members understand their roles and responsibilities as employers?			
32 Does the committee follow a systematic procedure in appointments?			
33 Do all staff and volunteers have an up-to-date contract and job description?			
34 Are all staff inducted into the organization?			
35 Do all staff receive training according to the needs of the organization?			
36 Do staff have a code of conduct?			
37 Is there an appraisal system?			
38 Is there a policy and procedure on equal opportunities employment?			
39 Is there a written pay policy?			
40 Is there a health and safety policy?			
Users			
41 Is there a statement and procedure on equal opportunities?			

	Yes	No	Action
42 Is a complaints procedure communicated to all users?			
43 Is all documentation produced in appropriate and accessible language?			
44 Are there agreed criteria for eligibility for the service?			
45 Are users represented on the management committee?			
46 Is there a clear procedure for initial and periodic assessment?			
47 Does the organization work to a set of agreed quality standards?			
48 Is there a clear charging policy, where appropriate?			
49 Is there a clear health and safety policy?			
50 Are statistics on usage regularly reported?			
Members of management committee			
51 Do all members understand the mission/aims of the organization?			
52 Do all members understand the constitution?			
53 Do all members know what documents comprise the constitution?			
54 Do all members know the areas and programmes of work?			
55 Do all members know the board's government and management structures?			
56 Do all members know the board's procedures?			
57 Do all members know the criteria for recruitment of board members?			
58 Do all members have a specific area of responsibility?			
59 Do all members understand their role in providing community leadership?			
60 Do all members have a plan for developing their own skills to support the work of the organization?			

INDEX